Copyright © 2019 Rebecca Trumbull.
All rights reserved. No part of this book may be reproduced or utilized in any form or by any means, electronic or mechanical, including photocopying, recording, or by information storage and retrieval system, without written permission from the author.

Design by BookCreate
Seattle, Washington USA

Printed in USA

ISBN 9780578508405

Disclaimer

This is my story as I remember it. I may have misremembered some details but none that are germane to the heart of the story.

Little As You Were

A life revealed

Rebecca Trumbull

For my children Bettina and Daniel and my husband Steve, the people who gave me the opportunity to create a family very different from the one in which I grew up.

1. Little As You Were

I fell off a cliff when I was six years old. My family was camping on an island at Lake George in the Adirondacks in upstate New York, our usual summer vacation spot. The morning sun was rising over the mountains to the east, burning through the clouds and capturing the mist rising off the still, silent lake. The ground, soaked with dampness from a thunderstorm the night before, contained clusters of pine needles collected where the rivers of rain had carried them. The glacier rocks covering the campsite were wet and slippery. My father, brother Ricky and I awoke early and walked out to the high point of a cliff that rose above the lake on our campsite. We loved looking out over the silky lake as the sun made its climb into the morning sky.

Huckleberry Island cliff

My father was smoking his pipe and looking out over the lake while Ricky and I explored. Before I knew what was happening, I slipped and fell off the cliff. As if lying on my back with my arms and legs splayed to a full Leonardo da Vinci Vitruvian Man pose, I fell the equivalent of three stories before I hit the water. Stunned, I did not scream or cry out. My eyes were wide open as I looked up and sank below the surface. I noticed the shade of blue of the sky. Not knowing how to swim, I was terrified. My brother told me many years later that it was he who said, "Daddy, where's Becky?" Only then, he said, did my father jump in, fully clothed, to catch me as I rose to the surface and hold me as we headed in to shore. This must have all happened in a split second but it felt like forever.

"There was never a moment's danger," my father proudly announced to everyone. "Good thing she fell into water; otherwise it could have killed her," I heard him say.

I don't think my father meant to lose track of me as I explored the wet, slippery rocks. He might have been thinking about the patterns the quiet wind played on the surface of the lake. Or he might have been thinking about the arc of the sun, and the relationship between the size of the sun and its place in the sky. He might have been creating the equation that would lay this out in a scientific way. These were the types of things he thought about.

"Don't get so close, Becky, I don't want you to get hurt," my father might have said, or "Becky, stay close to me, honey, I don't want you to fall." But he didn't say anything, and I fell off the cliff and it was my father who saved me from drowning. As I look back on my childhood, this incident is the first I recall of what would become a common occurrence: my father was unable to consider events that might come about in the future, including an empty gas tank or a stop sign. He often blithely drove along a country road, slamming on the brakes when a stop sign seemed to appear out of nowhere. He lived in what these days might be called "the moment" and failed to anticipate what might come next. This left my mother burdened with all the possible options, a responsibility which allowed her to fill in the blanks with horrible, fearful outcomes. My brother told me recently that as a two-year-old toddler clad only in diapers, he left the house, where my father was caring for him, and wandered off in search of my mother. Only when a neighbor found him, blocks away, and returned him home, did my father realize he was gone.

The fall off the cliff was my earliest recollection of a moment that left me with the sense that my father would not be there for me to prevent falls off cliffs or in life. That moment I began to feel precariously balanced, delicately perched, a sensation that has never left me. Going forward, I would soon discover, I was on my own. I had to watch out for myself.

Even my father could not have anticipated the much greater tragedy that was to come. My fall off the cliff would soon be all but forgotten.

Peter and me

The person who unabashedly adored me was my brother Peter. A black-and-white photograph taken for a special occasion, perhaps Easter Sunday, captures the two of us. It is one of a series of photos my father took of us against the blossoming quince tree. At sixteen, Peter is dressed in a suit with a very narrow lapel and even narrower tie. His dirty-blond hair, parted and combed carefully to the side, is reminiscent of the new president, John F.

Kennedy. Deep-set eyes and a graceful upturned nose highlight his soft cheekbones; his grin is slightly off center as he leans in towards me. His handsome, square hands reach down to my shoulders, and I beam with pride as he holds me close to him. I am dressed in a light-colored coat that covers my white dress with blue smocking. An elegant ballerina bun has replaced my everyday braids. My smile reaches almost to the deep dimples in either cheek. We are really celebrating Peter's new front tooth, white again after the sickly gray color it became following a collision with a lacrosse stick. At six, I am aware of none of this except that my adored big brother is back home with me.

It was I who would be cut out of the photo for the obituary.

My parents, Bettina and VanVechten — known as Bet and Van — staggered their precious two-week vacations each year. My mother went first, taking a vacation from her job as legal secretary at the surrogate court in Schenectady, New York. My father followed, taking vacation from his job as a writer and editor for the General Electric Company. Lake George was a short drive from our home, allowing the non-vacationing parent to join us on the weekends.

Each year they collected the moldy, musty, green canvas tent and piled all five kids into the station wagon. With the car packed to the gills, I climbed into the "way back" and straddled the camping gear as we began the hour-long drive.

Lake George was the most special place in the world: the place that we all waited for, dreamt of, longed for, year after year. It was a place of unmarked time, of sunny days and sunburns, of card games, of good long books, of endless swimming in the crisp mountain spring–fed lake water. Each day the sun rose over Black Mountain in the east, warming the air and drying the ground from the night's dew. Reaching its midday high point, it then arced its long way down over Tongue Mountain in the west and, finally, settled in for the night.

Lake George mornings held the promise of the day: I would wake up with the sun, sleep in my eyes, and unzip my sleeping bag on the now-deflated air mattress. Pulling a worn and faded red sweatshirt over my pajamas, I would climb barefoot from the tent and make my way across the hard-packed ground to the picnic table, where pancakes or hot oatmeal were being served. My father would hover over the rusty, green camping stove, occasionally pumping the pressure tank to keep the gas flame lit for the duration of the meal.

At 9:30, the tour boat Mohican would make its morning pass by our island. "Becky!" Peter said one morning. "The Mohican! Let's go wave hello!" He took my hand and ran us to a rock outcropping at the water's edge, where we waved, our ritual salute. The ship captain honked his horn in return and passengers waved to us.

Lake George nights almost always included cozy campfires with s'mores and songs, stars glittering in the sky, and the occasional treat of northern lights or a midnight swim. My favorite nighttime activity was "bark boats." We collected small pieces of bark, attached birthday candles to them, lit the candles, and sent the little boats out on a calm quiet lake. I loved watching the flickering candles as the little "boats" were taken by the gentle wind.

To me, Lake George was perfect. Of course, I never had to worry about battening down the hatches when the fierce winds tore through the night. Amidst the ear-cracking thunder and dramatic lightning, when the torrential rains came, I fully believed that I was safe and dry.

As a young girl I was aware that my family was special. Our hometown newspaper ran an article, "Scholarships Run in Trumbull Family," about the three eldest siblings: Jonathan, heading back to Harvard (whose tuition was $1,520); Nancy, starting at Radcliffe; and Peter, off to Philips

Academy at Andover. My mother must have been especially proud as several years earlier, when my brother Ricky was born, she, recalling the Down's baby my father's sister had delivered, told the doctor, "If this is a Down's baby, I don't want to see it. Ever." Imperfection was intolerable to her. Blessed with three perfect children, all of whom had scholarships, and two tag-a-long cute younger children, my parents were both proud of and grateful for their abundance of good fortune.

My family was divided into two parts. Trumbull Family Part 1 included the three older accomplished and polished siblings. Trumbull Family Part 2 included my brother Ricky and me, the younger ones bringing up the rear. The two parts of the family never lived all together full time because the oldest ones were all off at boarding school and college.

When the older siblings came home for a visit, though, I loved being witness to the hum of activity in this big messy family. Friends always stopped by and my parents welcomed them all, making large dinners that included passionate talk and the warmth of friendship. Voices overlapped in a cacophony of sounds, and I heard words and names like "existentialism" and "Kant" and "H. L. Mencken" dropped into conversations, few of which I understood. There was always music playing on the "hi-fi," usually classical or musicals, often opera, and sometimes Henry Mancini or the Kingston Trio. Neighbors opened their Schenectady Gazette year after year to see each of our portraits used in advertisements for the best portrait photographer in Schenectady. "Let me take your child's photo and he might look as good as this!" the ads might as well have cried out. Once when Peter was home for the Christmas holiday, he, Ricky, and I posed for a photo to grace the cover of Sealtest's Northeastern News wishing our favorite milkman, Art, a happy New Year.

With everyone home for the holidays it was a loud and lively family. Passions lived on the surface and temper tantrums thrown by one family

Sealtest cover

member or another sprouted throughout the house. They often involved the single bathroom. "Goddamn it, you chowder head, get off the throne!" my father screamed at Jon as he kicked in the locked bathroom door, knocking it off its hinges.

But we were special. And I loved being a part of it.

Peter was confident and charming and he knew it. He was comfortable in the spotlight on a stage and equally as comfortable as a star on the lacrosse field. "You could drop Peter out of the sky into an unknown place and by evening he would have friends, a place to sleep, and a good meal," my mother would say. But Peter also had a profound rebellious streak; he was always pushing the envelope. Did he do this in reaction to his older siblings who followed a straight and narrow path? Was he suffocating in the shadow of their perfect report cards? Did he sense they were too burdened by the rigidity of their accomplished lives that they forgot to enjoy themselves? Or perhaps his sense of confidence outweighed anything else, and he simply believed he could do anything and did not deserve to be held to others' rules. His exploration of life outside the rules was evidenced in the letters we read long after his death. We found letters from Gary, the assistant choir master at his church, love letters from a twenty-year-old young man to a fifteen-year-old boy. Was this abuse, not unusual in the church as we have recently come to discover? Or did Peter reciprocate the love? The letters that Peter wrote this young man are lost, but Gary's letters to Peter promise a ring to express his love, a ring that was on Peter's finger when he died. Gary died, in his early 40s, in the 1980s, with no cause of death given in his obituary.

Peter grabbed the wheel of life and steered in the direction he wanted to go, determined to enjoy himself. Not satisfied being one of many singers in the choir, he brought his pitch-perfect voice as head chorister and soloist for the St. George's Episcopal Church choir. In the letters we uncovered after his death we learned that he belonged to the "69 Club" at the church led by the Choirmaster. Its members included sopranos, altos and baritones, all young men.

Running in the house after choir rehearsal, Peter swooped me up in his arms, singing as he twirled me around, "How's my favorite little Becky?" Practicing some ballroom dance step with me in his arms, he whispered, "You are the best dancer of all!" If there were a lead part in a play, he always seemed to nail the audition. In awe as an endless parade of girls arrived at the house to see him, I always wondered how he convinced them to bring his little sister along on a date to the county fair.

Peter was also very smart. At four, while he was doing gymnastics on the railing of the front porch, my father called out to him, "Peter, what's one hundred thirty-six plus six hundred eighty-seven?"

"Eight hundred and twenty-three!" Peter shouted back after he completed his loop-de-loop.

"Peter, how did you do that so fast?" Uncle Eddie asked.

"Count. Real. Fast," he said.

In an essay written during detention in junior high — evidence, no doubt, of living well — Peter stated, "I want to go to a prep school, and then on to Harvard." The top scorer of all eighth-graders throughout New York State on a standardized test, Peter was soon pursued by Andover which offered him a full scholarship. A perfect match — an elite prep school and Peter, the son who would not be tamed.

Early in his freshman year, the letters began to arrive. The warnings were sent directly to Peter and copied to my parents. His first transgression was flinging butter on the ceiling of the dining hall. Only a month later, he was caught sneaking out of his dorm room window to meet a girl from a neighboring boarding school. He managed to avoid trouble for the rest of his first year and returned for his sophomore year, but the rebellion started anew. In spite of my mother's pleas to him in letter after letter — "Andover and a good college and you've got it made, Pete!" — in the spring of his sophomore year he was expelled for the final allotted transgression: smoking a cigarette in his dorm room.

Peter returned to the local public high school when he arrived home. To me, he seemed better than ever; he brought his sparkle, bustling energy, and the bounce in his step that I loved so much. Not a week went by before he won the lead part in the school play. Betsy Campbell, Wendy Stuart, and Tina Bueche, some of the girls he had kept warm with letters while he was away, all came to the house to visit; did he also see Gary? That summer he landed the part of Tony in *West Side Story* at the local Light Opera Company. I could hear him singing "I've just met a girl named Maria" from the bathroom and I wished Maria were my name. Not missing a beat, Peter dove back into his life.

The grown-ups, I knew from overheard conversations, were sick with worry about what would become of Peter. They were preoccupied with his ability to craft a future after being given the heave-ho from what would have been his path to academic stardom.

That summer Peter had attended the funeral of a friend killed in a car crash. He arrived home shaken by the service and sickened by the open casket. Critiquing the event, he outlined for my mother exactly what he would have wanted had it been his funeral. "I would have been cremated and had a funeral service at St. George's," he pronounced to my Unitarian mother. The program for the memorial Eucharist for Peter Freeman Trumbull includes each of his requests, including hymns #345, "The King of Love," and #590, "Ten Thousand Times Ten Thousand," and Kyrie from the Mass in C, although it is not clear whether it was

Mozart's, Beethoven's, or Schubert's.

An eighth-grade essay entitled "Plans for My Future" outlines Peter's young dreams. "I would like to be an organist for a cathedral in Europe, perhaps Westminster Abbey in England, playing for the Queen and other Royalty . . . and when I get to be 75 years old, I plan to retire someplace in Europe and devote the rest of my life to composing music and designing organs for church music."

These dreams might have become reality except for that other side of Peter, the one so aptly captured in the business cards he and his friend Chris had professionally printed: "PETER TRUMBULL — Occupation PLAYBOY — Paris, France."

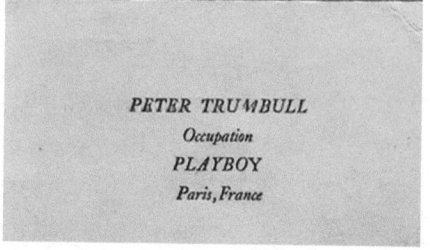

And except, of course, for the fact that he died.

The Lake George vacation of 1962 was to be quieter than those of the past, with only the Trumbull Family Part 2 on the campsite: Mom, Dad, Ricky, and me. Peter had to stay home to rehearse for West Side Story and would join us in a few days. My older brother Jon would have been with us except that, on the way to the lake, he and my father got into one of their temper-laden arguments about nothing particularly important, probably about stopping for cigarettes. "Just get out of the car and go home," Van might have yelled at him. And Jon did, hitchhiking his way back home. Nancy had left on a boat a week earlier that would take her to France, where she would then head to Paris for her junior year of college.

Smith's Boathouse, on the shore of Lake George, awaited us that summer, as it did year after year. Crusty old Fred and Clara Smith rented to us, for a dollar a day, a wooden rowboat to which we attached our own six-horsepower motor. My father referred to the boat as "the Trumbull yacht." I stood off to the side watching as the grown-ups carefully packed the boat with all our gear. Even today I can taste the Creamsicle and smell the leaded gasoline that filled those moments of eager anticipation before we headed out on the lake.

From Smith's, we took off for a cluster of islands known as the Narrows where the park ranger would assign us a campsite. Boating by the elegant and luxurious Sagamore Hotel meant we had left civilization behind. The hotel's bleached-white grandness and magnificent semicircular colonnade stood in salute as we puttered by. Its manicured lawn presented a smattering of chaise lounges coddling well-coifed vacationers. "Those poor people," my father said year after year, "have to stay in a hotel." We fell for it, hook, line, and sinker.

I loved the names of the islands that dotted the lake, names like Floating Battery, Hen and Chickens, and As You Were. My favorite was Little As You Were. It might have been a little sister, like me, to As You Were.

Ranger Biff always saved us what he considered a "prime" campsite. We sought a site with high ground and large sweeping glacial rocks that glided into the lake water, and a site speckled with sun and shade. My parents paid the ranger the fifty-cent per day rental fee, and we were ready to head to the campsite. That year Biff assigned us to Huckleberry Island.

We meandered slowly south on the lake in the heavily loaded boat, occasionally dipping our arms into the water. Our view was cradled by the cascading mountains

The Trumbull yacht

that reached down both the east and west shores of the long narrow lake, each new mountain overlapping the next, disappearing into the vanishing point.

"Let's make fast work of this!" my mother called out when we reached the dock. We carried equipment up to the campsite, set up the tent as shelter against a possible storm that might arrive out of nowhere, and found the kitchen supplies and the peanut butter and jelly. Through it all, we anticipated the hard and cool lake water — the most delicious water in the world — and the first swim, always the most special.

I counted the days until Peter's arrival; I knew that he would swim with me, sing with me, and best of all, hold me in his lap during the campfire. He made me feel like I was the only little sister in the world. Peter took care of me.

On that August Sunday in 1962, Peter and his friend Chris arrived at Smith's and rented their own speedboat. Like cowboys on bucking broncos, they twisted and turned the steering wheel of their boat as they came into shore at Huckleberry Island. Standing, wind blowing against their faces, they waved and shouted to announce their arrival. I ran to greet them as they pulled up to the dock. Peter stepped out of the boat as if he were stepping off the cover of a Kingston Trio record — hair closely shaved on the sides and back, with the distinctive little curl at the front. He tossed me in the air in his usual big hello. Then he hugged and kissed everyone and chattered about the news from home — how rehearsals were going, the girl he met the day before, and, finally, the shocking news fresh off the black-and-white TV from home: "Marilyn Monroe is dead."

"Why don't you boys take a swim?" my mother suggested joyously. "I'll have lunch ready for you when you come out."

"Beat ya!" Chris yelled, and they dove in for their first swim of the season. They were racing, Peter with his graceful athletic elegance, and

Chris sporting a rotund belly. No one knows for sure what happened next. All accounts indicate there was no specific event. Peter didn't hit his head nor was he hit by anything. The doctor who tried to resuscitate him told my parents it must have been heart failure. Desperate for clarity, my father requested an autopsy. The yellowed three-by-five notepad on which my father took notes from his conversation a week later with the medical examiner who conducted the autopsy says: "no cerebral hemorrhage . . . no heart attack . . . no injury to skull and neck . . . no water in lungs . . . not from mouth to mouth . . . both lungs bronchial pneumonia . . . feel but cannot prove-laryngeal spasm . . . no clear airway back through." There was never any clarity. Today I am convinced that my brother Peter died of hypertrophic cardiomyopathy, the most common cause of sudden cardiac death in young athletes. Not even given a name until the mid-1960s, and with the most common first clinical manifestation being sudden death, I am certain it was not something to which the Glens Falls Hospital had been exposed and would have known to look for during the autopsy.

But on that August day, all any of us knew was that Peter was swimming, and then, suddenly, he was hanging on the edge of the dock with his head cocked back at an awkward angle.

I curled up in the Army-Navy Surplus store hammock hung between two trees a short distance from the dock. My arms hugged my knees to my chest. In my well-worn, once-red-but-now-pink sweatshirt, swinging slowly and breathing in that unforgettable smell of pine trees, I watched as if the events, seemingly highlighted by the bright sky and crisp air, were surrounded by a large dark frame. Peter's hands gripped the edge of the dock, his head was flopped back, and he gasped for air. Everything was silent; there were no loud voices. I watched as my father pulled him out of the water and lay him down on his back on the dock in the beating sun. My father tried to find a pulse, and then, performing a Boy Scout routine he had practiced many times, tilted my brother's head back and breathed into his mouth. As he breathed his short — and then long — breaths into Peter's mouth, my mother entered the frame, kneeling down, rubbing Peter's arms and legs. "You're OK, Pete, we love you, Pete, please . . . I love you," she pleaded.

Huckleberry Island is a long mile from shore. Frantically waving down fast boats, we were mistaken for friendly folks waving hello. A ranger's boat finally stopped and approached the dock, slowly and carefully. I continued to watch, huddled, as they transferred Peter into the boat, my father continuing to breathe into his mouth. They sped off while I sat in the hammock. I only remember my own arms hugging my curled-up and silent self, watching, watching.

I stayed in the hammock, maybe falling asleep, for hours before my parents returned on that August day. My mother stepped out of the boat as if she were a queen, placing one leg delicately up and over the edge of the boat onto the dock where her son had lain, still alive, not three hours before. "Peter's dead," she announced with a frozen voice. I understood exactly what that meant, and I was only six.

What I did not understand that day was that my childhood, as I knew it, was over.

2. Sled-on-Wheels

"Well, that's the way it goes!" I said several times on the long drive home that August day after Peter died, according to a letter my father wrote recalling the details of the day.

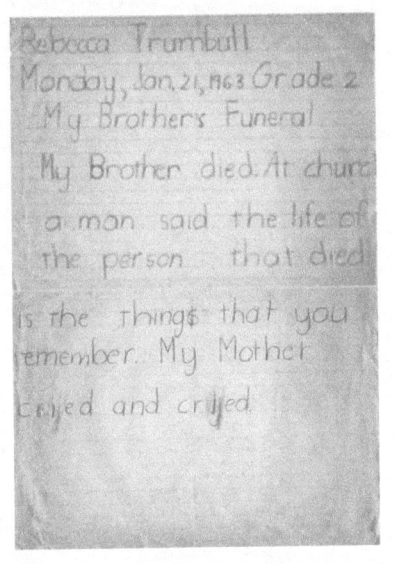

My Brother's Funeral

The house we returned to was empty and quiet; Peter's room was achingly silent. My older brother Jonathan would soon arrive home and learn the news. My sister was incommunicado, still *en route* to France; my father would deliver the news to her by way of a letter that she would receive when she reached Paris. We must have had some supper that evening, although I cannot recall what nor can I imagine eating. My mother gave Ricky and me sleeping pills. The medicine took effect and, tucked into our bunk beds on the sleeping porch, we fell asleep — Ricky on the top bunk and me below.

No seven-year old child should have to write an essay entitled "My Brother's Funeral," even if it is a chance to showcase beautiful handwriting. Children, in the world in which I grew up, seldom experienced unexpected death. They might, perhaps, lose a grandparent, an event more in keeping with the natural order of life, but no one I knew had ever lost a sibling. The teacher's comment? "What a nice story, Rebecca." Nice? Really?

Did I think the other four children would close in on the empty space created by Peter's absence and the family would somehow become whole again? Did I believe that we would simply transition from being a family with five children to a family with four children? I am not sure what I thought, but if I ever thought any of those things, I was dead wrong.

The five of us

Don't misunderstand me: I did not have a lousy childhood. I have many fond memories, but they seldom include my parents. I didn't know any differently, as I had no comparison. Only in retrospect do I realize that my challenge was far greater than that of many other children who cherish being thought of as an adult: I needed to learn how to be a child, to reclaim a childhood that had been wrenched away from me in an instant.

By the time I turned seven, a month after Peter died, I mastered what these days is called "executive function." I choreographed our family life, surreptitiously. My parents were both miserable. Their misery was compounded when they were together and only slightly more bearable when apart. With the overarching goal of maintaining peace in the house, I managed to keep my parents separated from one another much of the time. This was mainly accomplished by suggesting an activity away from the house with only one parent.

"Daddy, don't we need some firewood?" I asked one Saturday morning.

"By God, I think you're right," he said. "Bet, we're off. We'll be back late afternoon." And my father and I left to spend the day in the country looking for firewood, he sawing and splitting the wood for the fire, and me carrying it, one log at a time, to the car. One day, finding my way back into the woods, I came upon my father standing, ax up and behind him like a baseball bat. "Stand back," he said, stopping me dead in my tracks. There it was on the ground — tongue flicking out, hissing, and very angry. "I'm going to catch this rattlesnake," he said. Early in my parents' marriage he had snagged a rattlesnake and was a hero for bringing home the five dollars awarded him for the skin. But I knew rattlesnakes were deadly. I ask myself now why my father didn't tell me to turn around and go back to the car, why he allowed me to be anywhere in the vicinity. But at the time I didn't question placing the capture of the rattlesnake above my safety. This wasn't the first — nor would it be the last — time that I was an afterthought to something or someone more important.

Some days, my father and I carefully gathered our old newspapers, tied them up with string, and took them, as well as the collection of clean and flattened cans, to the recycling place. Sometimes my father and I went skiing in nearby Vermont. One Saturday, driving home, a car ran a stop sign and plowed into ours. Long before the advent of seat belts, my head flew into the windshield and blood dripped down my face. Grown-ups surrounded the car, including a man from the Texaco gas station across the street. My father got out and spoke to the other driver and the police while the Texaco man cleaned the blood and took care of me. Their ad had a jingle "Trust your car to the man who wears the Star…" and from that moment on, I loved Texaco gas station attendants who wore the star.

If I wasn't able to separate my parents, weekends were ripe for long arguments or day-long silences. Or my father sat, hunched over a libretto, following along with the Saturday afternoon Metropolitan Opera on the radio. He sobbed, in the distinctive way men often do, choking to muffle any possibility of really crying. "Becky, this is one of my favorites. Come listen," he said, encouraging me to come closer to him. I sidled up to him but never heard music; all I heard was his choking to try to keep himself from crying. To this day, I loathe opera.

My mother and I went together to the Salvation Army or to Loblaws Supermarket but our favorite outing was to the library. My mother despised librarians — she hated their persnickety rules and their rigid, tight-lipped personalities that, she believed, prevented more people from enjoying the library. But she loved books and weekly library visits were an important part of our lives. One librarian, Dorothy Brown, did not make my mother's skin crawl, and it was to her Brandywine Avenue branch that we headed every weekend. My mother always walked in with a large stack of books that she had read cover to cover and left with an equally large stack of books. Not much of a reader myself, I loved searching for books and carrying them home, thinking I might finally read one.

"Becky," my mother said to me one Saturday morning. "I have sad news. The Brandywine Library burned down last night." We drove over to see it. The smell of smoke filled the air and the ground was still slushy with a mixture of ash and water from the fire hose. Standing together, we held hands and looked at the charred remains of the building, with half-burned books still precariously perched in the window display. I recognized *The Story of Ferdinand* from the red cover and the drawing on the front.

Why did it have to be our favorite library that burned? What would happen to Mrs. Brown? Why couldn't it have been another branch of the library? For that matter, why couldn't it have been some other family whose sixteen-year-old had died? Who — or what — made these choices? Were they random? Or was an ultimate power or some mighty purpose at work in the universe? I began to think we must have done something wrong to be punished like this.

Seizing the opportunity to cry together, we stood there, holding hands. During some moments alone with my mother I felt an unbreakable bond that I could not put my finger on. It was an ineffable connection. I could never capture it as it was untouchable and I could only ever experience it fleetingly, as if in a dream. That day, we cried and cried, our shoulders heaving with a tortured rhythm in an unfamiliar intimacy. Someone passing by might have mistaken us for a mother and daughter crying over the loss of a person rather than a building or books, both of which were, of course, replaceable. I did not know then that my mother was grieving for so much more than a library.

I never read books as a child because I could not relax enough to allow myself to take my eye off the ball. With my antennae up and alert at all times, I was always looking out for the seeds of an argument and how best to position myself. I could not possibly have allowed myself to delve deep into a book, to lose myself even for a moment. And of course I could never measure up to my sister and her love of books. But I knew, though never said it, that I needed all my resources to ward off the next battle. Inside my home I could not be a child. There was no room for anyone's needs but my parents' and I learned very early in my life how to sublimate my needs to those of others. I learned how to disappear.

Evenings at my house were the worst, especially weekday evenings when it was impossible to keep my parents apart. My mother usually got home first and poured herself a glass of Almaden white wine in a small orange juice glass. My father followed soon after that, often giddily drunk, having finished a fifth of vodka on his walk home from work. If he arrived home sober, he was silent.

One evening, standing against the fireplace hoisting her skirt up to warm her rear end, a pose for which my mother was famous among their friends, she said, "Van, did you pay the electric bill?"

"No, I forgot."

"You didn't forget. You were too damn busy drinking the vodka, you bastard. Why couldn't you do the one thing I asked you to do? Why can't I depend on you?" What she really meant to say that day was, *Van, why didn't you save our precious son? Why couldn't you have done the one thing that would have spared me this pain? Van, why can't you be the kind of husband I could love?* Putting down her wine glass on the mantle, she picked up a fireplace log from the stack of newly chopped wood and hurled it at my father. He stood, unflinching, as it hit him in the forehead. I watched, unflinching, as blood poured down his face.

Evenings without a fight were dead silent. You could hear a pin drop.

Most evenings, after dinner, my mother went up to her room, closed the door, lay down on her bed, and cried. My father sat in the red chair in the living room and read. Every wall in our house was covered with bookshelves that my father had built. Each was painted white on the outside and a dark green on the inside, and each shelf had two complete rows of books, one in front of the other. He often lost himself in the pages of the Encyclopedia Britannica.

My brother Ricky escaped to his bedroom, formerly Peter's room, in the attic. Sometimes I went to his room and closed the door and we talked.

"Becky," he said one time. "You know that Peter might have lived but he would have been a vegetable? Mom and Dad

Ricky and me

thought it would be better to let him die."

"What? Peter could have lived? He would be home with us now?"

"But, Becky, being a vegetable means he would have sat in a wheelchair all the time, drooling, and wouldn't have been able to talk or eat or sing or do anything. Can you imagine Peter like that?"

"Nope, I can't. Yuck."

All of this was pure fantasy, but since no one talked to us, we talked to each other, and, at eleven and seven years of age, we were swimming in misinformation. Maybe Ricky overheard someone say that if Peter had lived, he would have suffered irreparable brain damage from being without oxygen for so long. With no real information to go on, Ricky shared whatever he heard with me, perhaps embellishing the facts. Adoring my brother Ricky, I worshipped most of what he said and did. But that is when I learned that nothing is as bad as what a child's imagination can conjure up. Peter, in fact, died soon after he was placed on the dock and my father began artificial respiration. Not detecting a pulse, my father continued to breathe into his lungs throughout the boat ride and the long ambulance ride, until they arrived at the hospital and Peter was pronounced dead.

Most evenings I was on my own. One night I knocked on my mother's door and entered her room. Sitting down next to her where she lay on her bed with her eyes covered with a damp washcloth, I asked her, "Could I be enough for you?" She just cried louder. I did not know then what I would learn decades later: not only could I not be enough for my mother, my very existence reminded her of all she had lost.

We did not utter Peter's name in our house. In the early 1960s people were not familiar with self-help books or tell-all television shows. My parents did what the extended Trumbull family had by then perfected: failing to say something out loud was license to believe it simply did not happen. Like everything else that no one in my family talked about,

Peter's death was one of a series of tragedies that filled the air we breathed. The silence surrounding his death left us with an irreparably torn fabric that we called our family.

Jews sit *shiva*, a week-long period after a death in which the family stays home and receives visitors who bring meals, stories, memories, tears, laughter, and photos. It is a time to recall everything one can about the person who has died. Adherents of Zoroastrianism, the ancient Persian religion and philosophy, ritually wash and dress the body and then lay it upon a clean, white sheet and place it in a tower where vultures come to pick clean the corpse. Judaism, Zoroastrianism, I would have welcomed anything that allowed us as a family to talk about rather than ignore the death of my brother. I wanted to pick clean the collection of memories in the same way vultures pick clean a corpse. There was a reason we could not say Peter's name, that we could not talk about him, but I would not learn until only recently what might have spilled out if we had opened that Pandora's box. All I knew as a child was that I could not say his name.

My father drowned his sorrows in drink and my mother directed all her anger at him. She wanted the unattainable knight in shining armor who would make everything all right, but instead she had my father. And he could not save her dying son. She hated him, in part, no doubt, because he didn't save her son. He failed to do the only thing that might have given her a reason to love him again. She detested the way he drank his tea very black, his buzz-cut haircuts, his disregard for his teeth. Did my father love my mother? I am not sure. He made overtures that indicated that he loved her, like bringing home boxes of Whitman's chocolates.

But he also did things that even I, as a young girl, knew didn't seem like affectionate gestures. Like the time he brought home a collection of snakes he had collected while out on a hike. "Oh Bet," he said, dismissing her concerns, "it's under control. I have them in a cage in the basement," he said. But they all escaped the jury-rigged top he made for the cage and we had eleven snakes crawling about the house. Of all my mother's fears, snakes may have been at the top of the list, followed closely by tunnels. If this was his way of showing anger towards her, why was he so angry? If it wasn't anger, what could explain this? Reminded of my father's generosity towards everyone outside the family, I began to wonder why his fury seemed reserved only for my mother.

I felt cheated as a child. Cheated out of a life with my brother Peter, my favorite sibling. By the devastation his death caused my family. That I had to live in a house filled with misery and bitterness, with a mother who clung to an earlier life and a father who drank his way into oblivion. But I never asked for attention because I knew there wasn't room for me.

Two recurring dreams plagued my childhood. The first had my family driving a fully packed car onto a very high bridge only to have the bridge disappear half way across, toppling all of us into the great abyss. The second was that I arrived home alone to an empty house, and upon opening the door, found that everything in the house had turned into tortoise shell, all hard, cold surfaces, with nothing soft remaining.

One evening my mother arrived home from work, following my father by a few minutes. She headed down into the cellar to feed the dirty coal furnace that she despised. On the way down she tripped over my father's boot with a fifth of vodka tucked inside. The house shook with her fury.

"Van, goddamn it," she yelled at the top of her lungs. "Why didn't you just finish the damn bottle rather than try to hide it?"

"Oh, Bet," he said. "Can't we just have a nice quiet evening?" His voice was quiet and meek in its drunken response.

My father's kind of drinking was not OK, I knew, because if it were, he wouldn't have had to do it in secret. When drunk, he didn't get angry or violent; instead he became placid and pleasant, pitiful and spineless. His quick temper, ready to pounce on something someone said, or erupt into a diatribe that far outweighed the importance of the topic, disappeared when he was drunk. I relished the lack of vitriol but I loathed the lack of authenticity, his ease, the smiles and laughter that came from a place that was not real. As a child, I imagined that all I needed to do was touch him with the tip of my finger and he would fall over. It reinforced my feeling that I could not count on him, that he might collapse in on himself if I needed him. But to hate him would have conflicted with my need for him, because he was the one who put me to bed each night and sang to me the songs I recall every word of today: "Grandfather's Clock," "Erie Canal," "I Ride an Old Paint."

But it was a war. And my mother and father were on opposite sides. Believing I needed to choose sides and recalling the ineffable and ephemeral bond I occasionally experienced with my mother which I never experienced with my father, I chose my mother's side. Even though she seemed to have no love left over for me, her youngest. The vodka and the weakness it produced in my father kept me from joining his side. This war had no winners.

There had been a time when my mother and father were in love with one another. This I know based on letters they sent each other while courting. In a letter my mother wrote my father, she said, "You have brought me more happiness, more tears, than any other man. I love you, need I say more?

Except that I love your smile…your eyes when I have done something you wish I hadn't…the way you talk…the things you say… your hands.

I ask nothing, expect nothing, want everything.

You have been wonderful to me.

I love you."

And a letter my father wrote my mother: "You are the most exasperating person I know, and the loveliest. You are sweet, beautiful, silly, dangerous, stupid, harmless, brilliant, good, bad. You can be wild and willful as a child and the next moment incredibly mature, with the insight of sorrowisdom (sic) and ages of tragedy. You exhaust all the adjectives. I can't put you out of my thoughts, yet thinking about you is a torment. It makes me want to write poetry, and I cannot. It makes me want to sing, and I croak. You arouse in me aspirations that I know I never will, that I cannot, fulfill."

His prescience might well have served as a warning bell.

Our home was not always somber and dark; it was only like that when populated with Trumbull Family Part 2. Fortunately, Jon and Nancy often came home from college, bringing friends who were welcomed with open arms and the house returned to its loud, messy, and happy state. Always ready to set another place at the table, my folks extended the meal and made up another bed. They loved the young adults, full of vim and vigor, who were eager to join in conversations. With guests, no one screamed or yelled and no one was angrily silent. The house sparkled with life, with laughter, stories, jokes, songs, music, and impassioned conversations that went late into the night. My parents much preferred the company of those old enough to engage in the kinds of heady conversations that appealed to them.

My sister and her roommate Becky visited during their senior year of college. The grown-ups were all excited about the genetic experiment Becky was conducting. She expressed a need for blood samples from several members of a single family. "We'll do it!" my father offered.

Terrified of needles, I yelled out, "No! I won't do that!" That night I awoke with my father and Becky hovering over me sticking a needle in my earlobe. Screaming with fury, I learned that day that it didn't seem to matter to my father if I said "no." It was dismissed, like so much else of me.

With only Trumbull Family Part 2, I can count on one hand the number of times my parents interacted with one another without arguing. These infrequent moments mostly involved my brother Rick's hair. My parents associated long hair with thugs and hoodlums. But the times they were a-changin', and we'd seen the Beatles on *The Ed Sullivan Show* and Rick wanted to grow his hair long. Smiling, I sat off to the side and observed the argument. My mother said, "Rick, no excuses. You need to get a haircut tomorrow. Here's a dollar fifty."

"Don't come home until your hair is short, Rick," my father added.

I was no angel. I learned early and did my fair share of stealing penny candy from the local market — my favorites were Tootsie Rolls and Mary Janes. I seldom misbehaved, though, because I was too busy trying to hold things together and I didn't want to be the reason everything fell apart. One day my best friends Molly and Cinda and I drove with our mothers to a local farmers market. Intrigued by the funny shaped things with bumps all over them, Molly, Cinda and I each took one, hid it under our coat, and placed it under the front seat of the car. Feeling quite smug, given our accomplishment, we were a bit taken aback when my mother started the car and gourds rolled out from under the front seat. We were had. Marched into the market, our mothers witnessed our admission and apology for what we had done.

Another time, my parents, Rick and I went to New York City, the only time we had ever gone to the big city, because my father wanted to see the Broadway show *Kiss Me Kate*. Exhausted after a long and tiring day touring the city, I whined throughout the show. My father had to take me back to the hotel early, missing Act II. Feeling guilty my whole life for having acted in what some might say is an age-appropriate way, years later I drove my father, partially paralyzed, wheelchair-bound and diaper-clad, from Philadelphia to New York City to see the reprisal of *Kiss Me Kate* on Broadway in the late 1990s. We clapped together at the end of each song, using his only functioning hand and one of mine.

The unhappiness in my family was tightly held within the family. The unwritten rule was that I was never to say anything to anyone about my family life. It didn't matter; if I were to say anything to anyone, it would promptly be dismissed and outweighed by sympathy for the loss my parents had suffered.

One day I said, "Mom. Why can't we ever be happy? Why can't we be a family like other families? They spend evenings together in the living room and don't argue with each other."

"Go find yourself another family if ours isn't good enough for you," she said.

Years before I was born, my father lost his job as an English teacher at a Schenectady public high school based on early college activity that had given him a reputation as a communist sympathizer. Whispers indicated that he had been a victim of a local Joseph McCarthy–like effort. I once asked him, years later, if he was a communist. "No, I am not," he said. "But I am a socialist." He brought those beliefs to everything he did, including the time he wrote the IRS, unprompted, apologizing for possible underpayment of taxes and enclosing a check. "Taxes," he said, "are the only way a capitalist society can spread the wealth around."

Not that my parents had anything resembling wealth. My mother was known for her "finds" at the Salvation Army, and for hanging up paper towels to dry and reuse. There was one bright shining moment, however, when she thought her fortune might change. My father was offered a faculty position at a college in New Hampshire, a position that would provide him with all the benefits of an academic life: professor's hours, summers off, and the inherent status, if not an abundance of money. I learned much later that the offer included tuition for pursuit of the Ph.D. in philosophy for which he strived. My mother never forgave him for declining this position. I can hear my mother singing Rosie's song from *Bye Bye Birdie*, "It could have been such a wonderful life / I could have been Mrs. Peterson / Mrs. Albert Peterson / Mrs. Phi Beta Kappa Peterson / the English teacher's wife . . ." Instead, my father took a job as an editor at the *Schenectady Daily Gazette*. Did he really prefer newspaper work at night to a faculty position at a college? Or, once again, was he expressing anger with his stubborn refusal to accept the position? He did have a passion for newspaper work, a fact born out years later when he worked a second job at the Washington Post alongside Carl Bernstein and Bob Woodward during the Watergate era. But was it truly his passion for newspaper work or did he want to get away from my mother and me every evening? At the *Gazette*, he worked nights while my mother worked days. Always looking for an excuse for their imploding marriage, my mother blamed those jobs and the two of them passing like ships in the night. Eventually he took a day job as a writer for General Electric, but by then it was too late.

My mother's education had been cut short when, only a few weeks into her first year at college, she was called home by her mother, who claimed she could not live without her daughter. Never returning to college, her sense of inferiority lasted her lifetime. With no higher education, her career options and associated salary were limited. She was a stellar secretary, and her bosses loved and appreciated her. When asked once by my Uncle Eddie if her fingers knew when she made a mistake, she looked up at him and said, defiantly, "My fingers don't make mistakes." A person of remarkable intelligence, at a different time and in other circumstances, she might have become so much more, but instead she was a legal secretary. To compensate, she read books. When given a chance, she read a book a day. Laser focused on topics and things that interested her, she read *A Room of One's Own* by Virginia Woolf, and then went on to read everything she could find about Virginia Woolf and the writers known as the Bloomsbury Group. She read all the published letters between each of the members of that circle, including Lytton Strachey and Vita Sackville-West, and any and all biographies she could lay her hands on. She wanted to *be* Virginia Woolf. Her job and her books provided her the only respite from the life she led, the constant reminders of all she had lost, and the life she would never live.

"I knew there must be 'something more'," my mother wrote in a letter to me as I was becoming an adult, "but I didn't know how to go about it. I wanted "out" and yet "in" of my situation…there were no women's groups or consciousness raising – we gals stood outside with our kids to keep them from being run over until you were old enough to play by yourselves…we talked about kids and recipes, books we were reading, things we wanted to do – but most of the time we didn't even know that we wanted to do something nor did we know of the things that could be done. We were too busy most of the time, too young, too satisfied and too dissatisfied to know about ourselves. Mostly we accepted."

I was eight years old when my sister Nancy arrived home from college one day. I ran in the house from playing down the street. Filthy from our tree-climbing adventure, Molly, Cinda, Priscilla, Cynthia and I hovered in the foyer to await Nancy's descent down the staircase. Our pre-pubescent adoring eyes peered out from our grubby little faces. I was the lucky one; I was the one with this wonderful big sister, this erudite and beautiful young woman, envy of all the girls, our role model. We stood, awaiting her arrival. When she rounded the corner of the staircase, she stood on a step about six feet above and ten feet away from us. That might be as close as I ever really got to my sister. And I was always looking up to her. Nancy personified perfection. It was not possible for me to have conceived of my sister as anything but perfect.

Only a couple years later everyone in the house pulsated with joy and anticipation of Nancy's wedding the next day. I am not sure there is anything more exciting to a ten-year-old. Friends and relatives arrived; nothing but happiness filled the house. Nancy, who graduated summa cum laude from Harvard (in the first class to receive diplomas from Harvard University rather than Radcliffe College), had met David the Harvard Business School student; tall and handsome with a square face and a deep laugh, he was a match for her beauty. They were, as my father liked to say, a sight for sore eyes. "Mom, you should hear his laugh," Nancy reported home when she first introduced him to the family. For my group of adoring friends, the object of our admiration had grown overnight from the divine Nancy to the divine couple, Nancy and David. David brought a new life to the family that had been missing since Peter died. He was funny and charming and he slid right into the Trumbull family. David brought joy and laughter back into the house. I loved him with all my heart.

David and me

September 12 arrived and the Unitarian Church awaited us. I woke up with a very sore leg — a pulled muscle from overzealous activity the day before. "She's just jealous, she wants to be the bride," I heard from behind closed doors. *They are so wrong,* I thought to myself. No one understood the impact the misery in the house had on me and I hungered for any occasion where my family might find some happiness. This wedding was no exception. I was too busy living a life of tree climbing and bike riding and wanted only to relish every last minute of the joy whenever given the opportunity. My father avoided

Flower girl

the dismissive response he and my sister typically directed at anyone suffering misfortune, "El tough-o," and instead humored me by wrapping my leg in an ace bandage and giving me a chair to sit on in the reception line. As flower girl, I joined the Maid of Honor and the bride in the one quirky feature of the wedding: we all wore blue shoes that had to be specially dyed for the occasion. Years later, it was much easier to find the blue shoes that I wore at my own wedding in a nod to my sister.

My single happiest moment in the years after Peter died was a visit to the newlyweds in their apartment with a fireplace at 52 Garden Street in Cambridge. I had never been in a home where evenings weren't filled with constant arguing, tension and fighting. I sat curled up on the sofa in front of the fire and watched as the evening unfolded, easily and comfortably and without silence or loud voices. I relaxed, and perhaps for the first time in my young life, I felt at home. Imagine my utter delight when a blizzard extended my idea of heaven an extra two days. David had entered the weekend with much trepidation, having never spent any time with a ten-year-old, but he fell as much in love with me as I did with him. "Weckie," he called me, to rhyme with Becky. Making them breakfast in bed one morning, I felt utterly accomplished. I still recall the overcooked scrambled eggs and cold toast.

Dinners at Garden Street were held at a table lit with candles and no television on in the background. "Oth," my sister said, using his prep school nickname created out of the first syllable of his last name and putting her hand on his shoulder, "would you like more?"

"Please," he said, and she poured from the bottle of French

Nancy by the fire

burgundy. "Pour yourself some and come sit down. I have news: I have been offered a position with the World Bank. It would require we spend two years in Colombia, South America. What do you think?" he asked, raising his glass towards her.

They continued their conversation and I registered the tone of their voices, the lack of anger, and the kindness. I remain grateful to them for providing my first glance, in that little apartment on Garden Street, into what a home might feel like.

Having seen Nancy and David's home life, my own, by contrast, became more unbearable. My brother Rick and I grew closer, enjoying moments of pleasure when the two of us were washing the dishes and singing "Georgy Girl," or "Alfie," always in harmony. Or heading out to see him, by now the high school's renowned actor, in his school plays. My favorites were *A Thousand Clowns* and *Life with Father*. Rick was "Father," and he was a good one.

The biggest thing that saved me, though, was Waverly Place, the street I lived on. That was where I could be a child.

Schenectady is one of three cities that form the Capital Region of New York State, or what is known today as the tri-cities. One hundred fifty miles north of New York City, Albany is the capital, Troy the manufacturing town, and Schenectady home to the former headquarters of the General Electric Company, who bestowed upon the city the motto "The City that Lights and Hauls the World," paying homage to the trains and lightbulbs that were produced there. A city ripe with history, it has neighborhoods to prove it: the lovely Stockade area, named for an early group of houses built by Dutch settlers and once surrounded by a wooden stockade, and today one of the most dense concentrations of seventeenth- and eighteenth-century houses in the United States; and the GE Realty Plot, a small early twentieth-century community built by the General Electric Company that contains a collection of stately Tudor, Queen Anne, Georgian Revival, Dutch Colonial, and Spanish Colonial houses on enormous lots with grand front porches and *porte cocheres*. Home to GE's highly paid executives, the GE Plot was laid out on gently curving roads with sweeping driveways and elegant trees.

As a child driving through the GE Plot or the Stockade, I would look out the window of the backseat of the car and imagine living in one of those beautiful houses. As I imagined the scene, my parents were in the kitchen, laughing and talking while making dinner, and I was happily playing near them, maybe a game of checkers or *Teeko*, our favorite board game, with my brother Rick. It was the picture of a happy family. To this day, I love peering into lit houses in the early evening and imagining who lives there and how they have arranged their space, their families, their lives. My greatest accomplishment in life may be that, in the several moves my family has made, I have had the opportunity to arrange and rearrange an unfamiliar space to make it into a home.

Waverly Place was a small and intimate street and I knew all my neighbors. It might as well have been Mayberry. Solidly middle-class, the neighborhood was dotted with modest but handsome early twentieth-century houses. My block, intersected by Rugby Road at one end and The Plaza, a pretentious name for an otherwise ordinary street, at the other end, had nineteen houses on one side and twenty-one on the other all packed tightly together on small lots. The street pulsated with children: one time we counted seventy-one children on the block. It was, after all, the post–World War II years and people were having babies as if they might go out of style.

Kids in the early 1960s seldom had organized activities after school or on weekends and we did not have homework. There was a lot of unstructured time. Every afternoon at three o'clock kids poured out of Elmer Avenue Elementary School and walked the two blocks to homes where mothers would welcome them. After grabbing a snack, everyone would head outdoors to play. Weekends were wide open, endless days of play.

Envious of other kids who told me "I can't play today; my family is going to Luray Caverns… or a Purim celebration…" I seldom had reason to tell friends that I couldn't come out to play because I was doing something with my family. I seemed to always be available. My parents were grateful I had friends who got me out of the house.

Whoever stumbled out of a house became part of that day's activities and groups were fluid from day to day. Molly and Cinda and I might drag out our crutches and hold a session of the Crutches Club. Envious of a girl at school who was on crutches, we found the wooden version at the local Salvation Army and created a club, comprised, I suspect, of the only three people in the world with this unique interest. We convened the Crutches Club whenever the mood struck us. We practiced and perfected a number of moves on our crutches, becoming quite facile with them. Building on the theme, we tore white sheets into strips to wrap around our legs to mimic a plaster cast. How could I, lost in my world of creating the perfect cast, be worried about what awaited me at home that evening?

Molly, me and Cinda

My home life and my life as a child on Waverly Place seldom intersected.

The Sled-on-Wheels might have been the single item that cemented my status in the social hierarchy. The Wechslers, family friends, had given me this gift. The Flexible Flyer Company was testing out a sled that ran on wheels and could be used in warm weather. Made of varnished wood and steel that was once painted red, its trademarked name was the Flexy Racer, but we all called it the Sled-on-Wheels. I may owe a lot of my childhood popularity to the Sled-on-Wheels. Cinda would sprawl on her belly on the rough wood, feet hanging off the back, her hands clutching tight to the two steering handles up front; I would pull her by a rope behind my bicycle. A fast block-long run was heaven. The speed itself prevented me from thinking about the upcoming evening at home.

Bea, Lew, and Nick Wechsler and the Sled-on-Wheels

There was no larger mission to the act of playing on Waverly Place. It would not make me a great ballet dancer, nor a gymnast, nor a musician, nor save starving children. It was pure play. It was creative and inventive. Sometimes it involved significant orchestration, including identifying players and arranging ourselves into leaders and followers. Then we played. Do not underestimate the amount of finesse that went into those endless days of play: we placated hurt feelings, shifted leaders if someone wasn't meeting expectations, and negotiated to keep players engaged in the game. I was a leader on Waverly Place and I stood tall and proud. This was where my life was good and successful. I felt confident, capable, and accomplished, feelings I seldom experienced at home. If my home life was hell, my world on Waverly Place was heaven.

Guilty, perhaps, for the miserable home life they provided, my parents decided to fix up my bedroom: refinishing the floors, wallpapering the walls, and giving me new antique furniture, including a heavy, dark mahogany four-poster bed. Their good friend Bill Murphy gave me a dark mahogany Victorian dresser on which I would proudly display my sister's wedding photo. It became the nicest room in the house, hands down. The wallpaper was a soft white with lovely large-scale pink and red flowers. The floors were bright, light-colored, and shiny oak; their smooth, silky finish was so different from all the other splintery floors in the house. By creating such a stark contrast with the rest of the house, my parents might as well have been saying, "This is the only place in the house where you might feel happy and good." And they probably also knew that while I loved my new room, I would happily have given it up for feeling comfortable and cozy in the living room with both my parents, without arguing, without silence. That would never be an option for me, though,

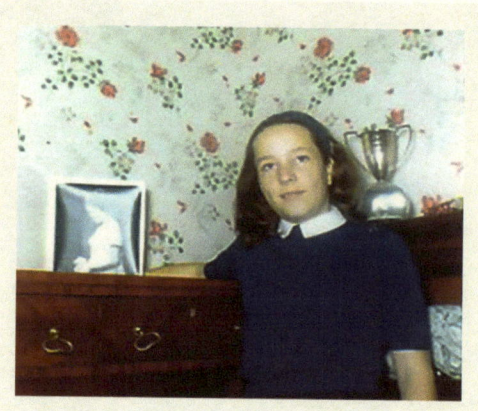

My new room

and it was to my beautiful bedroom that I often escaped. Mrs. Hope, my piano teacher, required that I practice the piano each evening for thirty minutes. But the piano was located in the dining room and sometimes I could not make my fingers work through the silence or the fighting in the house as I sat at the piano. I wondered what it would be like to practice the piano in a happy household in the GE Plot.

I gave up the piano and took up the flute. The mobility of the flute allowed me to practice in the privacy of my beautiful bedroom. While practicing, I would imagine the home life I would build someday. In the comfort of my room, I often practiced for much longer than my required thirty minutes.

In the years after Peter died, I was single-minded in pursuit of my goal. Only slowly starting to realize I had little sway over my parents' behavior, I focused my energy on imagining that, someday, I would create a home that looked very different from the one in which I grew up. Children will and should incorporate their own experiences, both good and bad, into creating their own lives. Contrasting my own sad home with the wonderful experience I had during my visit to 52 Garden Street, I began to collect data. I created a long list of things that would, and would not, be welcome in my home. The following were forbidden: TV during dinner; evenings of tortured silence in the living room; opera music that made people cry; throwing items at people, like a log for the fire or a wine glass; and loud voices. Alcohol, I decided, would be confined to a glass of red wine enjoyed at the dinner table rather than swigs taken from bottles hidden in the basement (this, taken so literally, meant that it took me a long time to develop a taste for white wine). My home, I decided, would include gestures like a hand on a shoulder or a tender glance. It would include the lovely unfolding of many evenings. It would always include splinter-free floors. And, finally, evenings in my family would not include blood.

3. The Snowy White Owl

My parents' friend Bill Murphy saved my life during the years after Peter died. After the funeral he took my brother Ricky and me to join his family at *Isabella*, the Murphy summer house in Nova Scotia, to escape our grief-stricken, paralyzed and silent household.

Perhaps Bill had become aware that my mother came home from work each and every day only to go up to her bedroom, close the door, and cry. Perhaps he knew — or had seen — that my father had taken to stopping at the liquor store on his three-mile walk home from work to buy a fifth of vodka and steal swigs in alleyways, hoping to deaden his pain. Did Bill know that Peter's death would irretrievably devastate a family that had once seemed so vital and alive? That this would be the tipping point for my mother? Did he know something else? Indeed he did, I now know.

Bill called Tottie, his battle-ax of a wife, "Mama," and, around me at least, he cowered in her presence, obeying her out of fear, not love. She pretended to be nice to me, but I never felt any warmth from her and

I kept her at arm's length. Bill, Tottie and my parents had met at the Unitarian church when each family's three children were six, four and two, long before I was born. My parents were the wannabe intellectuals, crawling up and out of their middle-class existence. Bill and Tottie, who had met on a blind date while at Harvard and Wellesley, were intellectuals with appropriate credentials. The two families became inseparable. The oldest sons of each family, David and Jonathan — with birth dates exactly three months apart — were well matched as oddball roommates at Harvard; the daughters of each family, Susan and Nancy, born exactly three days apart, were inseparable friends; and, finally, the youngest two, Chris and Peter, whose birthdays were exactly three weeks apart, were best friends. It was Chris who was swimming with Peter when he died. Bill placed a tremendous amount of importance on the coincidental connections of these family birthdays.

The Trumbull and Murphy families, long before Ricky and I came along, were intertwined in a way that is hard for me to understand today. They shared their lives. The two mothers and six children took off for *Isabella* for several months every summer. "The two mothers raised all six of us children," Chris told me years later. By the time I came along, they no longer shared summer vacations, but the families shared most Saturday evening dinners with the family of Sam Stratton, our local congressman. Much of the conversation was political, both local and national, all of them sporting various shades of the label "liberal democrat." And I recall many holidays and picnics together, all filled with words and wordplay. These events were busy and loud and filled with heady and often heated and stimulating conversations. My father, usually quiet and reserved, became animated around the Murphys. Bill, arriving at Washout Road for a picnic, would announce upon getting out of the car, "Event-wise, the trip was without!" Someone always found the opportunity to shout and mispronounce "cata-STROPHE!" about some event, and laughter followed. During a Saturday evening dinner and game night, at which Bill drank only orange juice, he and Ricky played our favorite board game, Teeko. Bill returned after a bathroom break to announce "I've just had an orange Teeko pee!" My father took the name of the opera, *Manon Lescaut* and transformed it into "Let's go, Manon!" — to holler when it was time to leave. Tottie participated equally in the intellectual conversations, offering her Wellesley bonfides whenever given the opportunity, but it was my mother, without so much as a community college degree, who brought a spark of life to a group of people. Everyone wanted to get close to her, the lovely and charming Bettina, with her big smile and warm heart. She had a way of making a person feel special, like the only person in the room, I am told. Her charm and warmth must have rankled Tottie, whose frequent reference to her high-end college degree must have gotten under my mother's skin. Underlying the close friendship between the families was serious competition between the two mothers.

The friendship between Bill and my parents endured until my parents died; the last letter my father received was from Bill, sending condolences for my mother's death. In a letter my father wrote all the kids, he says, "Bill stopped by on his way from the airport. We had a wonderful dinner of cod and steamed carrots, and he spent the night with us to break up the trip home. He and I stayed up late into the night, talking. What a wonderful friend he is." The friendship with Tottie did not fare so well, and Tottie barely tolerated the get togethers of the two families late in life. Eventually my mother refused to visit the Murphys, saying that she could no longer bear being in Tottie's presence.

I entered second grade the month after Peter died. At my school kids went home for lunch every day. Everyone lived within walking distance and would be greeted by a mother who had lunch ready. My parents both worked full-time so often I walked home and entered the cold, dark silence of my empty house through the unlocked front doors. Opening a can of Campbell's Chicken and Stars soup and heating it on the stove, I would sit down in front of the TV to watch the Donna Reed Show before heading back to school.

Three times a week, though, I had lunch with Bill. I walked the block and a half from Elmer Avenue Elementary School, marching down side-walked streets, eyes to the ground, no doubt, as I focused on the stone I was kicking along.

My Girl Scout uniform

Arriving at Bill's house, I climbed the wide wooden steps and walked across the porch encircled by a railing of white square posts that I imagined as a march of soldiers, with what I now know to be narrow tongue and groove flooring. I then reached a set of overly tall twin oak doors with large panes of beveled glass; my short fingers could barely make their way around the enormous brass doorknob.

Hearing the doorbell, Bill appeared through the beveled glass — the warm and glowing lights of the house backlighting him — and threw open the door to greet me. Grabbing my face — one hand on each cheek, almost suffocating me, he said, without fail, "Reb-e-QUAH (his pseudo-French pronunciation of my name) you are more beautiful than the last time I saw you. How can it be?" And he would give me a big loud, smacking kiss on my cheek. Fortunately, I seldom saw Tottie as she was off at her job managing a drug and sex education program for a local school district. In retrospect, it may be that the days she was at home were the days Bill and I headed off for lunch elsewhere.

Why did my parents allow and perhaps even encourage these lunches with Bill? Were they grateful I was not home alone, in an empty house, having a can of Campbell's soup? Did the lunches with Bill assuage their guilt for working all day? It was clear to me that my parents were no longer interested in the company of young children by the time I came around. At the time I thought they were simply grateful to Bill that someone else was handling this part of the parenting for which they didn't have the energy or wherewithal. Perhaps, in fact, this was an arrangement, anointed by my parents and eagerly anticipated by Bill. An arrangement that partially accommodated the truth surrounding the situation, the truth that I would not learn until my early sixties, eighteen years into the writing of this memoir.

But when I was a child, Bill was as good as a member of the family to me, given the closeness of the two families, and it wasn't hard for me to enjoy the lunches in spite of the underlying discomfort that occasionally arose in me about them. But given the contrast between the lives my classmates lived, with their mothers awaiting them at lunchtime, and my own life, with both parents working all day, I never found a good reason to challenge the situation. So the lunches continued, one after another, each perhaps more lovely than the last, and nothing ever went awry. Every time Bill greeted me, I wondered what on earth I could have done to deserve such attention. Squirming at the use of the word "beautiful" in relation to me (a word often used to describe my sister) I didn't know how to respond. But I never wanted to ask why we had these lunches and why he paid such attention to me because, underneath any discomfort I might have felt, I also felt loved, an unfamiliar and nice feeling. It might have been Bill who taught me that I could be loved.

Sometimes I arrived at Bill's in my school clothes — a cotton dress with a white Peter Pan collar, buttons up the front and a gathered waist, the skirt falling just below my knees, and scuffed brown Oxford tie-shoes with well-worn soles at the bottom of my naked legs. Other days I arrived in my Girl Scout uniform, complete with badges methodically applied by hand to the banner draped diagonally across my chest. Always a dress, as girls were not allowed to wear pants to school. Bill often took photos of me during those lunches and years later enlarged a couple and gave them to my children. It is those photos that remind me of the clothing I wore. Bill was the person who took the most photos of me as a child. His daughter Sue, years later, said "I think Dad loved you more than any of us. How many photos are there of you sitting at the kitchen table?"

A portly fellow, Bill's snug button-down shirts disclosed to the world his appreciation for the beer he had grown to love during a sabbatical in Germany years before. Every year he would provide the status of the brewing session undertaken in Nova Scotia the past summer, where labeled vintage bottles were stored on rickety shelves in the basement, awaiting their grand opening the following summer. He talked to me as if I were an adult, a heady feeling for a young child, and he infused the conversation with life lessons. His soliloquies often began with him clearing his throat, a tenor-sounding snort, a sniffle, and a swallow, a professorial sound, I thought at the time. A lesson about alcohol came when Bill told me, "When I was thirty-five I swore off alcohol and I haven't had a drink since." My puzzled look, given that we had just discussed the nuances of beer, begged for an explanation. "Hard liquor is one thing," he told me, "but beer is in a different (implying acceptable) category." I registered this information, even as a seven-year old, and wondered where wine fell on the spectrum.

The button-down shirt, usually blue, was tucked into khaki pants with a belt that sank down below the curve of his expansive waist. Upon standing, he would put both hands in his pockets and jingle the loose change, a sound I love to this day. The chest pocket was always filled with Scripto mechanical pencils of different widths and lead types, from which he carefully selected the appropriate pencil needed to help make a point. Holding the pencil, he wrapped his thumb and forefinger, each with hairy middle segments and large white fingernail moons, around the top to twist the lead out. After writing the critical information he needed to convey, he then replayed the entire thing in reverse, twisting the top of the pencil in the opposite direction, and clipping it back into his pocket.

Occasionally, we drove to Maurice's Sandwich Shop where we sat at the counter. Bill always ordered their special: extra rare roast beef on an onion roll, and he would introduce me, proudly, to the owner of the shop, Maurice himself. That might be where I learned to say "Nice to see you" in my most grown up and polite voice. It is also where I learned that if something tastes good, you might as well eat two of them.

Most days Bill and I stayed at his house, where the smell of academia began to fill my nostrils upon entering the foyer. How does academia smell? For starters, it smells like time to have lunch with a little kid; this, so very different from my own parents who were at work all day. And the books — perhaps too many books — the musty books, and the piles and piles of paper, and references to Shakespeare that seemed to fill the air. It was sharp, salty, and filled with beer brine. I loved academia and all the warmth it provided then and would provide in the future.

We sat at the kitchen table in the nook, with the big picture window framing the view to the birdfeeder in the postage stamp backyard, and by then the smell of the chicken noodle soup had overpowered the scent of academia. Not high end, this chicken soup. Lipton's, I suppose, from a box. But Bill added extra noodles, just for me. Sitting across from one another at the table with its red checked plastic tablecloth, Bill bestowed upon me another nickname: "Beck-a-noodle." His son Chris shortened that to "Noodle," the name he calls me to this day.

Beck-a-Noodle, at the kitchen table

What on earth did we find to fill our lunch conversations? Lots of words and wordplay. As an English professor, he often expressed great dissatisfaction with the quality of the students and their inability to write a grammatically correct sentence. In a letter I received years later, he wrote, "'I did tell someone last summer that I taught a dead language, and, when pressed to reveal what it was, answered, 'English.' Certainly the language I studied and pretend to teach is not the one I encounter in America."

A friend who had attended the college where Bill taught, said, "You know Professor Murphy? Wow. He gave out C's to those who did well, B's if you did a really great job. A's," he said, "were reserved for God."

During our lunches, Bill would often quote a Shakespeare play or sonnet. He recounted the colleague who could recite from memory any passage from Homer's Odyssey if given the leading sentence. As Bill began to consider retirement, he bandied about the idea that he might memorize all of Shakespeare's sonnets. In a letter to me, he wrote, "Two lines from an early sonnet always come to me when I think of you and your mother together:

'Thou art thy mother's glass, and she in thee
calls back the lovely April of her prime.'"

The lighter side had Bill quoting Dorothy Parker and Ogden Nash poems, limericks (restricting it to clean ones for the most part) and many jokes, puns and word play. One day he said, "Becky, today I'm going to teach you some French," and he pulled out one of his mechanical pencils and wrote on a piece of paper, "Pas du le Rhône canú." He encouraged me to say it over and over until finally I realized I was saying "Paddle your own canoe," and we laughed. During

Bill and me

those years my personality began its unique and distinct dichotomy. Bill set me high on a pedestal, believing — and often telling me — I could be and do anything I wanted with my life. At home, I was mediocre at best, compared to my sister, and was told I had three career options to which I might strive: secretary, nurse or teacher. It was a constant battle in my own mind: was I or wasn't I good enough? I never questioned why Bill was so good to me. Why should I have questioned it? I didn't know any better; I didn't know that men don't typically host young children at their house for lunch several days a week. It was a time before the horrific stories of child abuse so prominent in the news today. At the time, I thought my company was a pleasant respite from the lousy students in the English department. I could not have imagined any other reason for him to lavish this attention on me.

Years later he wrote to me, "My definition of the best schoolroom in the world is Rebecca at one side of the table, WMM [as he referred to himself] on the other, and a bowl of noodle soup in the middle — with WMM as the pupil."

For me, these lunches were meals where, for once, someone focused on me. I wasn't quite sure what to do and I retreated often to silence. But Bill pursued me and kept at me until I began to feel an inkling of being worthy of attention. A note found among Bill's papers after he died, written in my five-year-old handwriting, said, "Dear Mister Bill, Do you like me? Thank you. I like you."

"Dear Becky," he responded on the attached note, "Yes. I like you very much. Mr. Bill." Words were central to our friendship, and often in the form of poems Bill wrote for me, some short and sweet and others quite long. Our lunch conversations and Bill's love of Strunk & White's *Elements of Style* influenced my writing from then on. I hope that today I am able to write a grammatically correct sentence.

Interruptions occurred constantly: "Becky, look!" he would say as he

> A Hope and a Prayer and an Incantation
> To RT from WMM
>
> Loveliest of girls, Rebecca, now
> With all my words I thee endow
> With hopes that you can use them better —
> So please sit down and write a letter.
>   For, if my one score days and ten
> Thirteen will not come again
> Here on Atlantic's Southern shore
> Where letters seem to come no more.
>   Had I an endless reach of time
> To beg your sympathy in rhyme
> I'd bend my every nerve and sinew
> If thus to make you write I'd win you.
>   But time, which passes swift as twinkles,
> Already marks my brow with wrinkles.
> If you don't write some letters soon,
> Suddenly 'twill be Tuesday noon
>   And you and I be gulping noodles
> Of which we'll oceans have and oodles,
> And fat we'll wax as any elephant
> Till letter writing seems irrelevant.
>   So please, before my journeys end,
> Let me hear news from my best friend —
> If of your grace you would delight me,
> Rebecca, please sit down and write me.

A Hope and a Prayer and an Incantation

pointed to the bird feeder, "a black-capped Chickadee" and, of course, when I turned to look I saw only a vague shape and some movement. As the last child in a family all of whom had perfect eyesight, no one ever thought to have my vision checked. Years went by that I would follow the direction of Bill's pointed finger, nod, and then look at the picture he would point out to me in the *Peterson Field Guide to Birds* to see what I had just missed; he kept a log, including date, time and location of all the birds that we saw — or more accurately, those he saw and I pretended to see. It took years before I finally got glasses.

Arriving at the kitchen table one day when I was nine years old, a long, rectangular green box sat at my place at the table. "It's a present for you, Becky. Go ahead, open it," he said. Inside was a wooden recorder, a flute-like musical instrument. Bill then pulled out a matching but larger green rectangular box from under the table that held the recorder he had bought for himself. "Shall we learn to play together?" he asked. He pulled out a book that provided self-taught lessons. Mine was a soprano recorder, his alto, and together we played duets.

By the time I started second grade, I had achieved a certain amount of notoriety due to the death of my brother a few weeks earlier. But it was a different kind of fame I experienced the day Bill arrived at the door of my classroom. People in Schenectady knew him from his various runs for political office. The day he arrived at my school he was known for the eulogy he wrote for Peter, printed in the local paper and entitled "Remembering an Unordinary Boy."

Bill gave his eulogy at my brother's funeral. "Peter…stood out as a Golden Boy. He had a natural effortless charm… Happily, however, Peter was no plaster saint…he was in and out of scrapes with dizzying frequency. He loved his fellow men; and he loved the girls too, sometimes consecutively, sometimes concurrently, usually the latter. And by the girls he was loved or hated, depending… Life in Heaven, now that Peter is there, is certainly not holier, but I'm sure it's a good deal livelier." My father, so grateful for words that rang true, sent Bill a note that said "I'm weary of acknowledging letters that assure me Pete is singing in the Heavenly Choir, a boy soprano again… More likely he would be stealing cigars and smoking them behind Satan's coal pile!" Bill's wife Tottie, Sue told me years later, asked Bill, "Would you have written something as beautiful if it had been for one of your own children?"

No one would have thought to question him, in his sartorial and professorial elbow-patched tweed jacket, when he took me out of the classroom. Heading out to his car, we drove straight to the Union College campus where a Snowy White Owl had perched on the limb of a tree and had waited, it seemed, for our arrival. Fortunately, an owl's large size allowed me a better fuzzy glimpse than I had ever had of a bird. What I could see that day, with crystal clarity, was how it felt to be plucked out of school by a lofty professor and taken on an unknown journey; now I was seen not simply as the kid whose brother had died. A different kind of notoriety shined on me that day.

But even Bill couldn't quite understand how bad things were in my house. One day I dredged up the nerve to say what I had kept quiet inside me for so long.

"Bill, my father is an alcoholic." He cringed. It clearly pained him to hear this.

"Oh Becky," he said. "Your father may drink too much but don't call him an alcoholic."

Silently I cried, *Bill, please listen to me! Please, I don't know where else to go, I need help, my father needs help, my family needs help! What do I need to do to get someone to listen to me?*

I learned then that even the most wonderful relationship might have its dark places, things not permitted or discussed. Only years later would I come to understand the secrets held between these two families. Could Bill's inability to hear me come from guilt he felt for the role he played in my family's grief? Did he play a role in the grief? At the time all I understood was that Bill, my ever-present friend, was unable to listen to or console me about my father and my life at home.

"Take this home to your parents. I think they'll like it," Bill said to me one day as he handed me a 3″ x 5″ photo of Peter and Chris standing in front of Bill's fireplace, taken when the boys were about ten.

Bill, I screamed in my head, *I cannot possibly bring this photo home to my parents! You don't know what it's like in my house — I can't say anything about Peter, I can't even say his name! If anyone says Peter's name, Mom bursts into tears and Daddy tries to comfort her, saying "Oh Bet . . ." and then she throws her wine glass or something at him and yells, mimicking his words, "Oh, Bet, nothing! Don't talk to me you despicable creature!"*

Silently, I accepted the photo, tucked it away, and took it home. Hiding it in my dresser drawer, I never shared the photo with my parents.

Peter's photo did not sit atop the mantle of the fireplace. No photo of Peter was anywhere on display. But that didn't matter. Peter was there, in every bit of air we breathed. The obituary photo of Peter at sixteen was seared into our visual fields. Even today when I hear a young mother express the desire to keep her child "this way forever," I always think, and sometimes say, "No, you don't. My brother Peter has stayed as he was in that photo, always sixteen years old. You don't want to keep your child in this moment in time; that means your child is dead.

Chris and Peter

You want your child to grow, to thrive, to live."

My father, fired from his job at General Electric (alcohol), found a new job in Washington, D.C. where we moved in 1967, five years after Peter's death. I was too excited about a fresh start to think much about missing my lunches with Bill or Waverly Place. I could not have imagined then how much I would feel the loss of not just the lunches but the bird-watching trips, the football games, the Christmas shopping ventures, the time Bill and I spent together. But Bill never forgot me.

A postcard of the Statue of Liberty arrived one day with a poem Bill had written for me:

> *A Nosegay of Rhymes for Rebecca*
>
> *I'm spending the day in New York,*
> *The tourists' magnificent Mecca.*
> *But I might be in Dublin or Cork*
> *For all that I see of Rebecca.*
>
> *She visits by lake and by mountain*
> *And might just as well travel to Siam.*
> *For her company I cannot count on:*
> *She is never, oh never, where I am.*

Long letters and frequent postcards, occasional telephone calls and infrequent visits kept our friendship alive. I have everything he ever wrote me in my possession: the poem he wrote me for my tenth birthday; the letters full of advice on life; the poem he wrote imploring me to write to him; and his long and impassioned advice on writing. "What delighted me most was your telling me about your interest in writing...I will be so proud when you publish your first book. And you will publish it too, and a second and a third..." Throughout my college years he and I occasionally met and he would hand over several hundred dollars in cash, saying "Not a word of this to anyone. This is between you and me." Another gift from those years is a book of Robert Frost's poems, which he inscribed with a poem for me. Throughout those challenging years, as I struggled with one decision or another, he often comforted me by quoting Frost's poem *The Road Not Taken* which concludes with the lines,

> "Two roads diverged in a wood, and I —
> I took the one less traveled by,
> And that has made all the difference."

As I prepared for my thesis work in graduate school, Bill begged me to write about a late nineteenth-early twentieth century Albany architect, Marcus T. Reynolds. Such a project would have brought me close to Schenectady where he still lived. Bill greased the wheels, introducing me to people who might advise me in my research about Reynolds. He might as well have rented an apartment for me. When my early research indicated that someone else had written "my thesis" on Reynolds, I switched topics, instead focusing on Sunnyside Gardens in Queens, New York, a fascinating planned community. Shame about his Queens, N.Y. roots prevented him from telling me that his own parents had lived in Sunnyside Gardens at one time.

I asked Bill to deliver a toast at my wedding. One verse reads:

> And, please, when Time, with passage sure, —
> That one disease that has no cure —
> Dims what is now a moment clear, —
> Think well of those assembled here —

*Of parent, sibling, guest and host, —
And him who offers up this toast."*

Soon after that I was the lucky recipient of one of his earliest and most awkward emails. I had never seen Bill uncomfortable with words. But email became a wonderful tool that provided us the opportunity to communicate quickly and often and sparked a vigorous reconnection. I learned more about his life as I grew older.

Bill, born in Queens, NY, was the first of his family to go to college. While everyone thought he was destined for City College in New York City (where he would have received a fine education, he was quick to point out), his mother uncovered a scholarship for someone named Murphy offered by Harvard University. Bill received the scholarship and attended Harvard instead. His first English teacher there, David Worcester, had an enormous impact on him and eventually helped him obtain his first teaching position at Harvard. When Prof. Worcester died of a brain tumor at age thirty-nine, Bill wrote a brief biography of him, distributing it to those who attended the funeral. Settling into an academic position at Union College in Schenectady NY, which offered him ample hours of free time, Bill set his sights on politics, running for both State Senator and State Assembly as a Democrat in a heavily Republican district. Although he lost both elections, through the process he met Samuel Stratton whose campaign he then ran (Sam won, and held the seat for thirty years). As an honor for helping with the campaign, Bill received a seat (unpaid, as he was quick to point out) on the public housing authority. There he met Jeanne Robert Foster who over the next decade would change the course of Bill's life. Jeanne Foster, he wrote in a piece about the craft of literary biography, "was a theosophist with belief in the ultimate power of some mighty purpose at work in the universe. She placed great significance on matters, strange and unlikely, which I thought mere coincidences." Mrs. Foster, as Bill called her in my presence, was enamored with Harvard after a brief time there. Bill's bona fides as a Harvard B.A. and Ph.D. recipient, as well as his time teaching there, helped to facilitate a friendship with Jeanne Foster. In time, she regaled Bill with stories about her great friend, John Butler Yeats, and expressed her desire to one day write his biography.

Early in his career, Bill began research into topics related to the Anti-Stratfordian theory, the idea that William Shakespeare was not the author of the work attributed to him. Bill emphatically sought to prove otherwise. Not once but twice when he was ready to put pen to paper, he opened the Sunday *New York Times* only to discover a review of "his book" written by someone else. Reflecting on this years later he said, "I was in my mid-forties and had achieved little — perhaps "nothing" is a better word — in either scholarship or politics."

Meanwhile, the friendship with Jeanne grew, and she learned that Bill's first child was born on William Butler Yeats' (WBY) birthday and his second son on the anniversary of his death. What might have been considered by others mere coincidences convinced Jeanne that Bill was to be the biographer of her friend, John Butler Yeats (JBY), father of the poet William. What sealed the deal, though, might have been Bill's piece on David Worcester which served as proof that he knew how to write a biography. She began to provide Bill with small "gifts" including original letters from JBY and before long she shared her vast collection.

Visiting Ireland, Bill met and charmed the Yeats family members (all except the poet's wife) who supported his efforts to write this biography. Only upon the death of the poet's wife did the materials, which she had fiercely guarded, become available to Bill. He spent the next ten and a half years researching, transcribing letters, writing, editing, and finally, producing a draft of his book that, considered too long, was rejected by the original publisher. Cornell University stepped up and agreed to publish the book but requested significant editing. My parents were instrumental in taking "the red pen" to the book, reducing its length by half (if you don't count the footnotes). As Bill would later say, his book *Prodigal Father* became, like Milton's hope for his own book centuries before, one that Bill hoped would "fit audience find, though few."

J. Paul Getty, Bill wrote, had a simple prescription for success: "Rise early, work late; strike oil." Jeanne Foster proved to be his oil.

"As I reflect on the past," Bill wrote, "I see so many examples of apparently haphazard events developing into parts of a fixed plan that I begin to wonder whether Jeanne Foster was right when she thought I was fated to write the life of JBY."

"Do you know what happened today?" Bill wrote in a letter I received for my twenty-first birthday. "Quite unplanned and in the normal course of daily work, I finished the last chapter of the unfinished book on which I have been working for ten and a half years. September 26…I am so happy about this day. You, not the bloody book — that I hardly know what I am saying." Oozing enthusiasm for the young woman I had become, he wrote, "How did you ever turn out so wonderful? Why do so many people love you? I don't know the answer to such philosophical questions…I am so proud of you that, as JBY said, 'I would thank god if I knew where to find him'… I think of you all the time."

Prodigal Father was nominated for the National Book Award. The winner that year, *Robert Kennedy and his Times*, was written by Bill's college classmate Arthur Schlesinger, who called to tell Bill that his book won only "because in this country the Kennedy name trumps all else."

Bill's second book about the Yeats family was entitled *Family Secrets*.

Bill often opined on what Jeanne Foster might have considered "a mighty purpose:" these coincidences that pile up, one on top of another,

Little As You Were

Cover of Prodigal Father

that might be part of a larger plan. His musings were often fatalistic and sometimes morose, often mentioning the short life we are given, and waxing poetic on how to make the best of it. His own mortality, and the responsibility he felt to have an impact with his life, weighed heavily on him. In a letter to me, he ended with, "Time, the only enemy, keeps nibbling away like rain on the Rockies and there's no way to stop him." He became the patriarch of a family with six grandchildren, one of whom was given the name Rebecca, and was clearly his favorite grandchild.

"You will be pleased and astonished by [her]," he wrote in a letter to me. "She is infinite cheerfulness, always smiling. She wakes up smiling, talks constantly, and has global curiosity — a marvelous combination of personality and intelligence. She reminds me very much of another little girl I knew long ago, also named Rebecca."

As my parents grew older and I was responsible for their care, Bill was my confidant. Days after their deaths, ten days apart, Bill helped me write an obituary for them. We got a quick lesson in how newspapers handle death announcements in the news. Accomplished people receive an obituary which might end up on the front page or deep in the recesses of the paper. Those less accomplished have to pay for what is now called a "Death Notice," which most definitely end up in the back. As I paid the bill for the Death Notices for my parents, Bill and I discussed the need for newspapers to make money however they could, and then, out of the blue, Bill asked me, "Do you think I will be obituary-worthy?" Together we laughed, considering how the newspaper gods make those decisions.

Bill helped me through life with both the mundane and the larger, more philosophical issues. We often discussed topics such as fate and luck, and nature vs. nurture. Bill was convinced that nature trumps nurture and that the personality arrives with the birth of a child and dogs him (or her) forever, for better or worse. "You," he said, were born with a delightful sunny personality, not a dark and foreboding one." Believing so strongly in nature, as he did, how could his gift to me, which could only be categorized at the time as nurture, have so significantly altered the trajectory of my life? Aside from the American Heritage Dictionary I received from him for my twelfth birthday, which I cherish to this day, he gave the child in me the most worthwhile gift imaginable: our lunches together and the palpable sensation of being loved.

Bill often commented on how lucky the Murphy family had been compared with the Trumbulls. As Bill and Tottie travelled the world promoting his work on the Yeats family my family suffered an onslaught of tragedies, each one perhaps worse than the previous one.

Five days before he died, Bill and I talked for an hour on the phone about the 2008 presidential election, his mind crisper, I dare say, than my own. "Imagine," he said to me that day, "what the American public will think if someone named Barack Hussein Obama becomes president?" He did not live to see that day. We talked about my children, of whom he was quite proud, and that day, for the first time ever, I said "Bill, I love you."

Removed from the email list Tottie used to inform people of Bill's death, I didn't know he had died. One day, a few weeks later, I opened the *New York Times* app on my computer for the first time ever. There, staring out at me was the front page (if there is such a thing on a computer) obituary entitled, "William M. Murphy, Yeats Scholar, dead at 92." I was devastated and shocked. A computer screen is not the way to learn of a loved one's death. Solace took weeks to come and it came in a funny way. The realization suddenly hit me: Bill had indeed been obituary-worthy, and in the *New York Times*! Looking up to the sky, I broke into laughter, sure that he was joining me in celebration that he had made the cut.

Bill died on my birthday, September 26, and his granddaughter Rebecca had his initials — WMM — tattooed on her arm.

4. Atticus, Hazel, and Maynard

My family's move to Washington, D.C. would mark, I hoped, a new beginning. Moving in the summer of 1967 for my father's new job, my parents insisted on living within the city limits, refusing, on principle, to consider the suburbs. They bought a house on Legation Street, rejecting a nicer house on Military Road because my pacifist parents didn't like the name of the street. We sold our house in Schenectady for $14,000 and bought the new one for $24,000. It was to be a fresh start.

We left so many things behind. My mother left some beloved furniture and her collection of antique dolls and I left Waverly Place and Bill. My mother tried to convince herself that she was thrilled to leave Schenectady and move her family to a cultured big city. I suspect she, too, hoped for a new beginning. Maybe the war between my parents would end. Maybe we would finally be a happy family.

The move gave me the opportunity to reassess my young life. Reviewing all the data, I became convinced I had been adopted. That was the only way I could explain why I felt less loved than my siblings. It also conveniently explained why I was not as smart as my older siblings, not as accomplished, and certainly not as beautiful as my older sister. It helped me understand why my parents could not find the enthusiasm for me that they found for my sister. Beginning to accept this view of the world, one day I discovered a folder of old letters, very carefully organized in chronological order, one of what I would learn to fondly call the "letter books." My parents kept carbon copies of all the letters they ever wrote and the letters they received in binders in chronological order; my father carefully recorded the beginning and end dates of each binder on the front. Inside was a letter from my mother to her friend Elisabeth dated May 1955, a few months shy of the day of my birth. In it, she said "Damn it, I'm pregnant again." Things could no longer be explained by my having been adopted and I became aware that my mother had not wanted another child. Very quickly I learned to envy children who were adopted; they, at least, were wanted.

A star in my social world on Waverly Place, I tried to bring that confidence with me to Washington. I failed miserably. Big city girls were shaving their legs, going steady, and smoking cigarettes. Having only recently learned how babies are made, I simply wasn't ready for this level of sophistication. Never having even noticed that I had hair on my legs, much less ever having shaved it off, I was thrust into a world where my appearance mattered. I had never paid one iota of attention to what I wore each day, unless it was to wear my Girl Scout uniform. Having been raised in hand-me-downs, the only new piece of clothing I recall from my childhood was a dress, in which I was wildly uncomfortable, bought for my weekly ballroom dancing class (a skill my mother was certain I needed in life). To this day, I still hesitate before wearing something new, having to convince myself there is no need to wait for a special occasion. In Washington, D.C., though, it soon became clear that my white cotton anklets would not serve me well. And I realized that I had to become interested in my appearance. I had no bell-bottoms, miniskirts, or makeup (especially white lipstick), and I didn't know how to smoke a cigarette. Unable to try these things one by one over a period of time, I devoured each of them, all at once, desperately hoping to fit in. I bought bell-bottoms, stole a stick of white lipstick from the Drug Fair, and asked Robert France to teach me how to smoke. My adored older brother Eric (as he was called by then) said, "Mom, let her shave her legs!" None of it worked. No doubt it didn't help that I showered using the only soap in the house — my father's homemade soap made out of bacon grease. I must have smelled like bacon.

The recorder Bill gave me was stolen the first week I arrived at my new junior high school in Washington, D.C., evidence of my lack of street smarts. Having stopped playing the recorder because I didn't have Bill to play duets with, losing the recorder itself was not a great loss. What I missed was the green box that served as its case. It was that green box that had sat on Bill's kitchen table in Schenectady when he said to me, "Go ahead and open it, Becky. It's a present for you," a moment in which my world felt full of possibility.

As my seventh-grade year wore on and my body grew outwards in a way that didn't align with Twiggy's, I hunched my shoulders more and more, hoping I could just disappear into the more comfortable place I once inhabited. Given and failing an eye exam, I got glasses for the first time. My mother took me to buy bras, trying to squeeze me into the smallest size possible, seemingly having ignored that I had grown quite a bosom. "Stand up straight!" she barked at me, constantly. I hated having breasts. The school dress code required that girls wear dresses or skirts, and the parental dress code would not permit me to wear anything that landed above the knee. Circumventing this rule, I simply rolled up my skirts at the waist, making them, in effect, miniskirts. But while other girls were wearing stockings, I was still wearing knee-highs. There was no way around it; I was a misfit. My only happy role was that of little sister to my brother Eric who had achieved status as the Big Man on Campus during his last two years in high school, his last two years at home.

Still reeling from the big urban junior high school, I was not doing well. In April that year Martin Luther King was assassinated. We watched on TV as riots broke out and fires burned throughout the city. As if replaying our visit to the library that had burned down, my mother drove me slowly by the charred remnants of a Cole Haan shoe store in a commercial strip on Connecticut Avenue near my house. This was my first real lesson in race.

My parents had long held liberal views and I received the appropriate lessons, such as watching *To Kill a Mockingbird* together followed by conversations about right and wrong and the choices Atticus made. Years earlier, my mother had refused an invitation to join the Daughters of the American Revolution because in 1939 the organization had denied the Negro singer Marian Anderson the opportunity to sing in their building, Constitution Hall; Anderson sang instead, and much more memorably, on the steps of the Lincoln Memorial.

In 1957, the Little Rock Nine had entered Central High School, an act many consider a turning point in school desegregation. The same year Bea and Lew Wechsler, of Sled-on-Wheels fame, had helped the black Myers family — Daisy, referred to in newspaper accounts as the "Rosa Parks of the North," and her husband Bill and their kids — buy the house next to them in Levittown, Pennsylvania, a housing development "for whites only." Bea and Lew fled to my family after they awoke in the night to the KKK burning a cross in their yard.

However much my parents could stand on ceremony when they made these political statements, though, I know my mother was afraid.

Weeks after King was killed, Robert Kennedy was assassinated. The country had not yet recovered from John Kennedy's assassination only five years before, and my family had not recovered from my brother Peter's death six years before. I was still trying to navigate my new social milieu while murder and death filled the world around me. Everything felt very shaky. We watched on TV as Mayor Daley's Chicago police unfurled batons on protesters during the Democratic National Convention. My parents, who had supported Gene McCarthy's candidacy and despised Hubert Humphrey, were repulsed watching the election returns in November of 1968 that announced our new president, Richard Nixon. "Nothing but a crook," my mother said as she imitated Nixon's *V for victory* sign, his classic pose. My pacifist parents became militant in their resistance to the Vietnam War, and our new home in Washington became ground zero for antiwar demonstrations. We welcomed protesters who slept on the floor and ate the homemade soup my father kept simmering on the stove. Youth was the only thing that would change the world, my parents had by then come to believe, and they loved the long hair, the rebellion, the headiness of the political statements. Politics infused our household. Black Power! Make Love Not War! Bring Home the Troops! Peace Now!

There were the occasional bright moments. The time Nancy and David came to visit with their year-old daughter was the highlight of my life. I loved Rachel in a way I had never loved anyone. It was free, pure and perfect love.

Rachel and me

Washington, D.C. chose 1968-69, my eighth-grade school year, as the year to implement busing as its solution to the Supreme Court's ruling years earlier to integrate all public schools. Black kids from poor neighborhoods throughout the city were bused to what had previously been all-white schools, often travelling over an hour to get to and from school. Few white kids were sent to predominantly black schools because their families had made their escape to the suburbs or private schools before the start of the school year. But not my family.

On the last day of eighth grade I returned my books, cleaned out my locker, and headed out to recess. Alone and looking for someone who might make me feel welcome, I stood out as a complete outcast, my shoulders hunched and face looking down. It had been another miserable year.

A gang of black girls, led by Hazel and Wanda, found me. They were big and had very large upper arms. Their kinky black hair was captured with lots of little colorful barrettes. Very loud, the English they spoke was not a language I understood. I recognized Hazel and Wanda from one of my classes. They were tough girls and I was scared to death. Someone tapped me on the shoulder from behind and, as I turned, fists came at me, and my glasses went flying, scuttling across the blacktop. I was petrified: loud scary voices are louder and scarier when you cannot see. "I got her!" one yelled, hurling more punches. I fell to the ground, writhing in pain.

"You're nothin' but white shit," one said as, hovering over me, she held her face inches from mine, with spittle coming out of her mouth. "You're trash, you're useless," she said.

"Help! Help me!" I yelled, but no one came. I was flat down on the ground, and very large and dark arms, large bellies, and knees were all over me. I was powerless.

I do not recall how all this ended. All I wanted were my glasses.

Still smarting from the beating the last day of eighth grade, I dredged up the nerve to return to school for ninth grade. Promising myself I would stand up straighter, I was determined not to be such a loser. But the very first day of school, at the same recess break, Hazel and Wanda and the girls showed up. As if an instant replay, the entire scene unfolded exactly as it had before. Once again, my glasses were thrown many feet and broken. Again, I do not recall how it ended, but I walked home with my broken glasses teetering on my nose.

My mother marched into the principal's office. "What are you going to do about this? This is unacceptable."

"We have no clue what to do," the principal said. "We have no idea how to deal with these kids. We are dumbfounded." I knew then that I didn't have a "pal" in my principal.

That evening, my brother Eric said, "You deserved to be beaten up."

"What? What did I do wrong? I am your little sister — what have I done?" I asked incredulously. Adoring and idolizing my brother, I was stunned.

"Because you're white."

I get it now. We had all bought into the larger political agenda and forgot about being human in the process. My family was pretty good at that. Eric could only see the political ideology while I could only see the whites of Hazel and Wanda's eyes.

As a family, we never talked about any of this. How could we? If we don't talk about, it simply won't be true. This incident conflicted with how my parents wanted to see the world, and race, and racial relations. For all the conversations about *Mockingbird*, whose lessons were neat and tidy and had offered a clear perspective on right and wrong, my situation was messy and it complicated all those same lessons. Without a way to discuss and process this experience, I was left with the last words spoken to me about it, by my own brother. "You deserved it. Because you're white."

When I refused to return to Alice Deal Junior High, my parents were completely flummoxed. Already holding a tenuous place at best in the family — I had never contributed what my siblings brought to the family: brilliance, talent, confidence, beauty — in addition to "unwanted," "school dropout" could be added to my long list of failings. I was reminded then that no one was going to keep me from falling off the cliff. I needed to chart my own way forward, no one was going to do it for me.

A bright spot appeared one day. My parents had an opportunity to buy a piece of property on an island at Lake George, where we continued to vacation even though it was laden with memories of Peter's death. They would buy the land together with Bea and Lew. We mapped out the location on USGS maps, a slice of Fourteen-Mile Island, named because it was fourteen miles north of the southernmost point of the lake. Imagining the house we might someday build there, together with the Wechslers, we all laughed as we more clearly imagined the tents we would set up for the foreseeable future. The sellers came back, however, saying "The deal is off. We will not sell to Jews." My parents might have circumvented the prejudice of the sellers, buying the place and selling half to Bea and Lew. But "no," my father said; he would not continue to negotiate with the sellers. And that is the end of the story. This was not the first time his high-minded moral stance got in the way of something that might have been wonderful.

Bridgette Bardot, my beloved cat whom we called BB, was my savior. I loved my big, fat tiger cat; she was always there for me. We took her with us wherever we went, even on vacations. One year we took off for Lake George, now a much longer drive from Washington, D.C. than it had been from Schenectady, and we took BB, as usual. She roamed the car freely; if cat travel containers existed in those days we certainly didn't own one. On the island BB was free. The trip home that year was a long one and we stopped at a rest stop. "Wait, let me get BB!" I called out before anyone opened the door.

"Nonsense," my father said. "BB won't go anywhere," and he opened the car door. BB jumped out of the car and ran off into the nearby woods. We spent the next several hours walking through those woods, calling her name, hitting a can of cat food with a fork, a sound to which she had always come running. BB didn't come back to us. We drove home through the night, another seven hours, and I cried the whole way home. Dropping Eric and me off at home, my parents turned around and drove the seven hours back to the same rest stop. Again they searched, stopping door to door in the nearby neighborhood, putting an ad in the paper, again calling out for our beloved BB. All to no avail. How easy it would have been for my father to simply let me hold BB before he opened the car door. I was furious with him.

"Why is Dad so stubborn?" I asked my mother a few days later.

"He is a stubborn man. Always convinced he is right. And he often is, Becky. For such a smart man, though, he often does really stupid things," she said. My mother had loved BB too, and we commiserated and grieved together. She then took the opportunity to impart a life lesson. "Is it better that you had a chance to love BB so fully even if you have now lost her? Is that better than never having been able to love BB at all?" She must be speaking from a place of authority on this topic, having loved and lost a child, I thought. Turning it over and over in my mind, I never was able to answer that question. What I now understand is that she was talking about so much more than BB or even her children.

"Becky! Help me!" my mother screamed. Eric had left for college by this time, and I was the only child remaining at home. Loud crashing, thumping, and the sound of breaking glass broke the quiet of the night. I ran to my parents' bedroom and flipped on the overhead light. The large ceramic bedside lamp was on the floor, shattered, while my mother stood to the side of my father who was lying in bed, his stiff body shaking uncontrollably. Foam and blood were coming out of his mouth. His head was tilted back. His eyes were rolled back into his head. He was unconscious. He made guttural-sounding noises. Certain he was dying, I called the operator. "Help," I said. "My father — I don't know what's wrong."

By the time the ambulance arrived, my father's first *grand mal* seizure was over and he was conscious and alert. Unaware of what had just happened, he brushed off the paramedics. "I'm fine and just want to go back to sleep," he said, "You can leave." Surrounded by glass and ceramic shards from the bedside lamp, my mother and I stood in disbelief. *You may think you're fine, Dad, but we're not fine. Consider us — we are the ones who saw this, we are the ones shaking with fear. You are not the only one impacted by what just happened. Damn you.* This alcohol-induced seizure was the first of many and the start of a long and painful period of life-threatening bad health, much of it self-inflicted. I held nothing but contempt for him and his self-absorbed neglect of his health. Sometimes I wondered if he just wanted to die.

"Dad," I said one evening when I decided to confront him. "You are an alcoholic. You need help. No one can help you but you. We'll be there for you but only if you get help. Look what this is doing to you and to us — you are falling apart. You'll be lucky if you make it to sixty at this rate."

"I drink," he said, "because of how you treat me. If you were nicer to me, I wouldn't drink." He got up, grabbed his jacket and the car keys and left. He drove, drunk, around the Washington Beltway, the sixty-one mile highway that circles the Washington, D.C. metropolitan area.

Being blamed was hard for me. Could the cause of my father's alcoholism be the way I treated him? I now know that is a classic response to confrontation with an alcoholic, but I didn't know that at the time. I questioned myself and him. Way too much responsibility was laid at my feet. Did I really deserve the blame for his alcoholism? What I knew was that he was ruining himself and I was never sure if he would live another year. Sometimes I didn't care and I begged my mother to divorce him. "I can't," she said, "I can't afford to."

My father was fired (alcohol, again) and got a job with the brand-new Environmental Protection Agency, a safe and probably boring government job that gave him good benefits and stability. Leaving there at four o'clock most days of the week, he headed to the Washington Post where he worked until midnight, arriving home in the wee hours of the morning, which allowed him three or four hours of sleep. "We need the money," he answered when I asked him why he did this. We may have needed the money but more than that, he loved newspaper work and the Post wouldn't hire him full-time, so he took what he could get. It was much more exciting to work among those investigating Watergate at the time. He, understandably, preferred that thrill and being at the newspaper to being home with my mother and me. I, in turn, much preferred the evenings alone with my mother. It was simply easier. I need to remind myself that I also despised my mother by this time. I loathed her for hating my father, for being so awful to him, for never being able to find a single good thing about him. If only she had found something good about him, maybe I could too.

Discussing arrangements to get to the airport for a visit I was making to a friend one morning, my father offered to drive me. "The car needs gas before you go," my mother said.

"We'll be fine," he said. My father and I took off that afternoon. On the highway, several miles from the airport, we ran out of gas. He stayed with the car to await AAA. There I was, fourteen-years-old, hitch-hiking my way to the airport so as not to miss my flight. It would have been so easy to get gas. Why did he need to ignore my mother's useful reminder that the car needed gas? Why did he seem to enjoy pushing things to the limit? What pleasure did he derive out of rejecting my mother's suggestion and seizing an opportunity to prove himself right (or, more often, wrong)?

In January of 1970, *Parade*, the *Washington Post* Sunday magazine section, ran a piece about the Hawthorne School, an alternative school started by Sandy and Eleanor Orr, husband and wife, who left behind their teaching positions at the prestigious Georgetown Day School. With tuition at $2,000 a year it was more than my parents could afford. Now I was not only not beautiful, brilliant, talented, or clever like my older siblings, I was about to become expensive.

I started at Hawthorne. "Hawthorne looks like Alice's Restaurant," the Parade Magazine said, "and the student body treats the Orrs like the Ray and Alice of the educational world. Everybody is on a first-name basis. There are few rules, no 'study halls,' bag lunches. Long before dress codes were relaxed in other high schools, Hawthorne students were grooving in and out of classes in mini-maxi-granny clothes, Army jackets, tights, sandals, beards and long, flowing hair." The school was comprised mostly of white hippies from middle-class families who for one reason or another did not do well in their local public school. I relaxed. I finally felt safe.

One day my mother called up to my attic bedroom, "Becky? What are you up to?"

"Studying and napping, intermittently," I responded.

"Well, you can't be that stupid if you are able to use the word *intermittent* correctly," she said.

I got a lousy education but I loved Hawthorne. I learned to make a dulcimer and a lot about Russian history and nothing about US history. My geometry class turned into a semester-long study of the philosopher Bertrand Russell. I was well-liked and had social opportunities I hadn't had in years. But this was the beginning of boy-girl relationships and all new territory. I rejected Quan-Yang who persistently pursued me, in favor of Denis Lachman who told me one day, "You are nothing special."

"I know," I responded. It was the one thing I accepted about myself: I was nothing special. I wouldn't have known what to do with Quan-Yang; he might have actually treated me as special, as number one.

The school made no bones of its strong political bent. During the Poor People's Campaign a few years earlier, the school opened its doors and the building overflowed with people sleeping on blankets, sleeping bags, and whatever they could find. It was at Hawthorne that I began to reconcile my political views with my personal experiences.

Soon finding itself in dire financial straits (in part because of their support of the Poor People's campaign), the Hawthorne School was given a last chance by entering into an agreement with the DC public school system that gave Hawthorne a building in exchange for educating forty-one public school students. The Sumner School building, now a National Historic Landmark and official museum of the DC public school system, was turned over to the Hawthorne School in September of 1970. Almost one hundred years earlier, this building was the first school built to educate Washington's black population. Abandoned by the school district years earlier, it was drafty and cold with peeling paint and broken windows. Hawthorne students didn't care, and it was there that I started the new school year with a student population of about one hundred kids, forty-one of whom were black. If I was ever scared, I don't remember.

One Saturday night I drove across town to the house of the school secretary, a lovely black woman named Nancy Williams, who had invited a number of students to a party. Entering her house, I joined right in, singing along with Al Green as he sang "I'm Still in Love with You." Nancy, pouring me a drink of soda, turned to me and said, "Becky, do you realize you're the only white person here?"

This is what I truly deserve, I thought to myself. *Here are my friends: Denise, whom we call Hutch, and Maynard and the others. I don't see them as scary black kids and they don't see me as "nothin' but white shit." I deserve to be judged not by the color of my skin but by the content of my character (thank you to Dr. Martin Luther King), and so do Hutch and Maynard and all the others.* In our little world of the Hawthorne School, in Washington, D.C., we succeeded.

5. Cherry Blossoms

Springtime in Washington, D.C., its most beautiful season, is warm and filled with blossoming fruit trees. In 1972 we welcomed our fifth Washington spring and things were looking up. My father's health was better, I was finding my sea legs socially, and there was a lull in national tragedies.

Bettina and young Jonathan

On one of those beautiful spring days, April 12, soaking in the fragrance of the dancing pink cherry blossoms out in full bloom along the Tidal Basin, I headed home from school. Once there, I looked up from my homework and saw my mother open the front door early. Way too early, I realize only in retrospect.

"Mom! You're home early!" I jumped up, shouting joyfully.

She stopped in the doorway, frozen solid in time and space, and said, to no one in particular, "Jon's dead. He committed suicide."

I ran to her and hugged her but she didn't hug me back; she might as well have been marble. No one hugged me until I arrived at school a couple days later and Sandy, the headmaster, greeted me at the door. He put his arms around me, silently, and held me while I cried. For a brief moment, I felt loved and comforted.

My brother Jonathan, who at thirty was a successful lawyer for the city of New York, had jumped to his death from his eighth-floor apartment in the Bronx. He didn't leave a note, but no one doubted he had committed suicide. Years later, we would posthumously diagnose him as manic-depressive based on symptoms that would by then become painfully familiar.

My parents left for New York that afternoon to identify Jon's body. Eric met them when they arrived but did not accompany them to the morgue. Just a few days before Jon died, the two had planned to have dinner. Eric called to cancel and Jon responded, "That's all right. I'm not much company, even to myself." Not only was Eric wracked with guilt, he was now the sole surviving son and his burden had, in an instant, become exponentially more burdensome.

Just as I had begun to get my young life in order, wham! Like water finding the path of least resistance, tragedy again found its way to my family. Ten years before, my brother Peter had died, and right on the decade mark, Jon killed himself. "Which one of us will it be in 1982?," I asked.

Oddly, I found a sense of comfort in the tragedy. It was familiar. Eric came home from New York to be with the family, and together he and I read the condolence notes that poured in, laughing at those who wrote expressing sorrow for the death of "Eric." I guess it was too much to ask of people to keep track of which Trumbull son had died.

I remember so little about my brother Jonathan. Even though he was in my life for many more years than my brother Peter, I recall so much less about him.

Struck by polio when he was ten, Jon almost died. The rest of his life he lived with one leg longer than the other, producing an odd gait. Intellectual and aloof, he was both physically and socially awkward and the least attractive person in the family. Rounded shoulders and a pot belly accentuated his nonexistent chin and disappearing lips.

With his scary temper, I knew from an early age to steer clear of him. Once, no doubt practicing my lettering, I made him a nice card and taped it to the door of his bedroom. spelling his name "J-o-h-n." He blew up at me, "Becky, my name is spelled J-O-N! Not J-O-H-N. Do not misspell my name again!" I got a breakneck lesson in the name Jonathan. Years later, I referred to a colleague whose name was "Jon" as "Jonathan." He responded by electronically yelling at me through email: "MY NAME IS JON, NOT JONATHAN!" I have done my best to steer clear of the name Jonathan ever since.

Jon attended Harvard and managed to graduate although it was not easy for him. Oblique references in letters suggest he had a nervous breakdown while there. I recall hearing conversations about Jon earning some money by volunteering for psychological experiments at the Harvard Student Health program. It was during those years that Timothy Leary was experimenting with LSD on students at numerous colleges, including Harvard, although records indicate the experiments were conducted only on graduate students.

With a few days leave from the Navy, his stint after college, Jon brought home a sailor named Tony who appeared to my nine-year-old brother Ricky, he told me years later, as effeminate. No one ever asked Jon anything about Tony. Outward signs indicated that Jon was obsessed with women, although his record with girls was spotty at best. At some point in high school he fell in love with a blonde girl named Judy Thalen, for whom he carried a torch for the rest of his life. Her photo was on his bedside stand when he died. Was she a ruse? Was she the "lady on his arm" when he needed to convince others he loved women? Was he a gay man way before that might have had a chance of surviving a family intent on outward appearances or the social mores of the 1960s? Or was he simply an unbearably uncomfortable person who could not seem to find love?

Jonathan was very proud of his name, Jonathan Trumbull, no middle name. It was the name of an early Connecticut governor and signer of the Declaration of Independence and, we believed, an ancestor. My parents considered a three-syllable first name with a two-syllable last name to have a poetic resonance. I, too, received a three-syllable first name and no middle name.

Post-Navy, Jon started law school in nearby Albany and moved back into the family house. His room was treated like a shrine. The door was kept closed and we were not welcomed in unless invited. He often lay on his single bed in the center of the room with stereo speakers equidistant on either side while he listened to Bach harpsichord music for hours on end. Once he invited me into his room; I was partially thrilled to be let in and partially terrified. He gave me half a Slim Jim.

Passing the New York State bar exam, he was hired for the position of assistant district attorney in New York City and announced proudly that his office was in the newly-opened World Trade Center building. He was an impatient and judgmental man, particularly towards those he believed inferior to him, so the job seemed perfect for him.

The last time I saw Jon, the Thanksgiving before he died, he arrived home sporting a foot-tall bong in the shape of a penis and testicles. Everyone laughed. On a long drive he spewed a monologue describing in detail a sexual encounter with a girl in which her legs were so high up they were tickling his ears. At sixteen, I cringed with discomfort.

He also proudly shared with the family a book of line drawings with imaginative machines and contraptions that also played the role of sex toys. One showed a machine that spun around and licked the genitals of the participant. Laughing, no one questioned his increasing obsession with sexuality.

Did anyone grasp that Jon had crossed a line? Did anyone think to question him? Many years later we began to understand that manic-depression often includes excessive interest in sex and inappropriate discussion of sexual activity in public settings. At the time, though, no one questioned his behavior. He was just "being Jon."

Religion had no place in my family. In a letter written to the Murphys while pregnant with me, my mother wrote, "Rick is going to Daily Vacation Bible School with [a neighborhood kid]. He loves it. Let them answer — Who made God? What is God made of? Is he all around, everywhere? Then you step on him every time you walk? Does he have a house? No? Well, what are churches for then? If he's in everybody's heart who took him out of the chicken's heart I just ate — or did I eat him?" Years later, my mother said, "Damn it, if there were a god, he never would have put me through so much suffering."

My father quietly maintained a spirituality that was never confined by the walls of a worship space or defined by certain melodies or rituals. It could be found in a sunset, dancing the hora, or singing to my children. In his younger and healthier years, my father would sit, pipe in hand, and watch the sun set over Lake George, the same lake where my brother Peter had died years before. The earth is turning, he would remind me; the sun is not going anywhere. "The Jews got it right," he told me one autumn. "This is a much better time for the start of a new year." As for Jesus Christ, he said to me, "He was a man, nothing more." Yet that awful day in August when we gathered to mourn Peter, we all found comfort in the trappings of St. George's Episcopal Church, sitting on the red velvet-upholstered pew cushions and listening to the choir sing. And years later my father walked with me, with a yarmulke attached to a few strands of silver-gray hair, down the aisle of Society Hill Synagogue where I was married. His absolute lack of connection with any particular religion provided him with a large palette of options although I am not sure that any one of them provided him with any real comfort.

My father also shared Kahlil Gibran's conviction, espoused in his poem *Your Children are Not Your Children:*

Your children are not your children.
They are the sons and daughters of Life's longing for itself.
They come through you but not from you,
And though they are with you yet they belong not to you.

Did this philosophy give him permission to disassociate from the deaths of his children? Or did he latch onto Gibran as a way to disconnect from his dead children?

Years later, when my parents turned eighty, they each suffered a stroke within days of each other. I was able to set them up in their home in Nova Scotia with round-the-clock nursing care. Enjoying a celebratory dinner the first evening back home, my father, slumped in his wheelchair but so very happy to be home, said, in his garbled English, "Let's call Jon."

"Jon who?" I asked, confused.

"Our Jon," he answered.

In my clarity of purpose, I said, "Pop, Jon is dead. Don't you remember? He died many years ago." Not yet acquainted with the addled brain of a person debilitated by stroke, I watched as he cried as if for the first time for the loss of his son.

I wondered then if he remembered when, decades earlier, we scattered Jon's ashes on Aunt Nancy and Uncle Eddies' farm in upstate

New York, site of many a wonderful Thanksgiving dinner, where only months before Jon had proudly driven the tractor around the fields.

That day I held my five-year-old niece Rachel as we scattered our handfuls of ashes. "Becky," she asked me, "will Jon grow into flowers?"

Jon on tractor

6. Dutchess

My sister had the most beautiful toes. No fat, stubby big toe with hair, like me. No, my sister Nancy had, until the day she died, elegant toes with handsome square nails that had never seen the underside of a coat of polish.

Nancy in Paris photobooth

Could I have ever imagined what would become of my sister, who I grew up to idolize, worship and imbue with perfection?

As a young woman, Nancy had an arresting beauty, a perfectly proportioned upturned face, with its gentle little nose, handsome lips, light-brown eyes, and graceful hair. She was striking in her A-line dress of Marimekko fabric in shades of brown and tan. Every word she spoke was carefully crafted and beautifully toned. She softened a's and deemphasized e's. Her accent was hard to place because she made it up. Its roots were British and French.

I could not have imagined my sister as anything but perfect.

Nancy often wore her chestnut hair swoopsed (a word my mother invented to describe the messy approach) high on her head. Picture *Breakfast at Tiffany's*: she looked like Audrey Hepburn with a twist. The shape of the head was important to her, and she pinned her hair up to accentuate the high point, elongating her neck and raising her elegant stature even higher. When I was twelve, and she a newly married twenty-four-year old, she stood behind me trying her best to swoopse my hair up into that regal look. Trying one thing, she examined it from all sides, sighed, and tried something else, her face drooping in disappointment. It was then that I learned the nuances of a nicely shaped head and that I didn't have one.

"Never look right at the camera," she said. "Look to the side, look away and up — it will add an element of mystery about you." Try as she might to impart these lessons to me, I learned only one. "Keep your voice low and throaty. A high-pitched voice doesn't sound elegant. And always gloss over the double 'e' sound in a word. It's grating on the ear."

Nancy, looking away

Dutchess County, New York was the source of the nickname given to her by my father. "Dutchess" seemed the perfect fit for her: regal and always slightly detached. If my father had ever given me a nickname after a county in New York State, it probably would have been "Herkimer," after its cheese. But he never gave me a nickname.

Nancy was to have been given the ancestral family name of Alcestis Kate. Instead, she was named for the beloved sister-in-law who drove my laboring mother to the hospital through a blizzard. My sister spent a good deal of time learning to accept her name, a certain disappointment.

Names meant a lot to her and there was a long list she didn't like. Kayleen topped the list of truly repulsive names; Linda she found banal and sophomoric, followed next, probably, by Maureen. "Kenneth," she said one day over a cup of coffee, "is a beautiful name. Not Ken, but Kenneth." Given the honor of naming me Rebecca when I was born, my sister had to settle for what she undoubtedly considered the second-best name of Rachel for her own daughter, after unsuccessfully lobbying her husband for the name Rue Morgan, a twist on the combination of the title of an Edgar Allen Poe story and a Parisian street name.

As an adult I learned that, just as I was taking my first baby steps, Nancy, at thirteen, started a daily diet of black tea and dates. She dropped to seventy-five pounds. My parents did nothing about it; it was 1956, after all, and I am sure they had never heard the word "anorexia." What might have prompted this? Today, this disease is often believed to be a reaction to a loss of control over one's life. Did my sister know something about the family over which she might have felt a loss of control? Did she detect something going wrong? Had she seen my mother being kissed under the mistletoe by someone other than my father and perhaps a tad too passionately? It was during that time that my sister adopted her new voice, the pseudo-British accent with a twist of French, and a brand-new personality, more reserved and distant. She abandoned her long-time friends, the ones I see in photographs with a healthy Nancy who still smiled for photos. Thin long before it became fashionable, she forged her own fashion sense: she led; she did not follow. She floated above others, never reaching down or back to be with those beneath or behind her. Her intellect was so far above and beyond her peers that she simply lived her life around them, finding companionship in the company of adults who could speak her language. A gifted student, she was wooed by a boarding school and soon after, by Harvard, who enrolled her on its dime before she had completed high school. She was a bright shining star with boundless potential.

A letter from my father awaited Nancy when she, only eighteen-years-old and a junior in college, arrived in Paris for a study-year abroad. "Dear Nancy, This is a hard letter to write… Peter is dead…" began the letter. Perhaps trumped today by the internet as the worst possible way to learn about a loved one's death, a letter, cold and inhumane, was the worst way possible in 1962. The family story might have played out differently if Nancy had returned home to be with us. Perhaps Nancy, the idolized daughter, might have demanded of our broken family the kind of comfort that we were unable to give each other.

Nancy, with cigarette, and me

Nancy adored Peter. But there was no word from her for several weeks. I can only imagine how tortured my parents must have been to think their daughter was so far away, alone and grieving. I imagine her wandering the streets of Paris, alone, agonized by her brother's death. Where did she turn for comfort? Did she want to come home? Family friend and local congressman Sam Stratton offered to help, using, as my father wrote in a letter to Nancy, "the good offices and resources of the State Department to reach you, wherever you might be, so we could talk to you on the phone and tell you about Peter. We said, "No thanks," knowing that Death was simply a fact that had to be accepted. We didn't want you to come home or anything like that. It was useless to waste money on long distance calls that would only provide the comfort we already had of having other human beings with us alive, sharing thoughts and memories, and assuaging grief in companionship." Was death really a "fact that had to be accepted" even if the person was his own beloved daughter, an eighteen-year-old far away and alone in Europe? Did he ever think about what kind of comfort the "wasted money" on a long distance phone call might have provided Nancy? Did he ever think to offer the opportunity to come home, even if it was something he didn't think was necessary?

The first letter Nancy wrote more than a month later was not to the family but to Bill Murphy, the family friend; it was found among his papers when he died. In it she writes, "At times on the street I see Peter. His slouch, his charm . . . the way he holds a cigarette, that's about the worst. . . Peter is okay. — I meant to write dead. But only for us that is bad. He is beautiful. Beautiful. Loved."

By the time Nancy arrived home a year later, my parents no longer spoke of Peter — he was dead and there was nothing anyone could do about it. We did not utter his name.

For the next several years, I saw my sister so infrequently that she was almost imaginary to me — an ethereal and lightly prancing figure always dressed, it seemed, in white and always with a cigarette hanging from her fingers. She had returned to Harvard by this time and whenever a letter arrived from her the house lit up with joy. My parents dropped everything — my mother even delayed pouring her ritual evening glass of white wine — to read the letter. My father carefully tore open the envelope, trying not to cut through any precious words my sister might have written. I hovered nearby as my parents hunched over the letter with a magnifying glass to decipher her miniscule scrawl. Using a fountain pen and ink, she wrote in the tiniest lettering to get the most out of each sheet of thin and delicate, usually airmail, paper. I loved evenings that included a letter from her. Dinner was delayed, sometimes significantly, while my parents happily captured every last word.

Nancy, in a white dress, and me

Was my sister's image of perfection — carefully crafted by her and encouraged by all those around her — simply too hard to uphold? Did the impossible task of maintaining this image lead to her ultimate downfall?

After two years in South America where Rachel was born, Nancy, her husband David with the great laugh, and their daughter Rachel made their home in New York City, where they joined Eric, a struggling actor, and Jon, Assistant District Attorney for the City. SoHo was an undiscovered and inexpensive area of Manhattan with cast-iron façades and trash dumpsters lining the streets. On the cutting edge of what would become a trend, they paid $12,000 and signed the papers to buy a loft. They opened the door to what, until that morning, had been a fully functioning sweatshop filled with seamstresses at their Singer sewing machines, attaching Calvin Klein labels to clothing. The only plumbing was a toilet with a pull chain. Nancy juggled renovations to the loft, raising a child, and getting a law degree, all while she and David made the loft into a home.

And what a home it was: exposed pipes ran underneath the creaky old windows and banged loudly through the cool fall evening. Outside was the cacophony of city sounds, and inside, opera music often played softly in the background. The expanded family now recreated the wonderful milieu to which Nancy and David had given life at 52 Garden Street in Cambridge years before. Dinners were held at the large, chunky, rectangular wood table. "Ave Maria!" Nancy shouted when she burned her finger taking the red cast-iron casserole out of the oven, setting the *Boeuf bourguignon* in the middle of the table. My sister had, indeed, mastered the art of French cooking using her first edition copy of Julia Child's *Mastering the Art of French Cooking* that she bought in France in 1962.

It was a dinner of that kind that Jon was to have enjoyed with Nancy,

David, and Rachel on Tuesday evening, April 11, 1972, after they were to return from a visit with David's parents in South America. But their flight was cancelled and they had no way to reach Jon to postpone the dinner. Arriving home the next day, they learned that he had killed himself. My sister crawled into bed, covered her head with pillows and stayed there for days. Jon was the only remaining sibling from Trumbull Family Part 1 and he was her closest sibling in both age and intellect. If the dinner had taken place, would Jon still be alive? At twenty-eight years old, Nancy's life was about to unravel. Was Jon's suicide the precipitating event? Or was this just the tipping point for her — the event that would finally undo my sister's sanity, which she had tenuously held together since Peter's death? Or since her days eating tea and dates? Was she seeing before her the complete dissolution of Trumbull Family Part 1?

I wonder if it is possible to reconstruct the elements of a demise, to pinpoint the exact moment when a different outcome might have been possible. Could there have been a time when, if she had turned left rather than right, or read one book rather than another, things would have turned out okay? Perhaps if she had been named Alcestis Kate or if my head shape had not disappointed her so. My whole family struggled to reconcile this beautiful and brilliant girl with the woman unable to get out of bed, feed herself, feed her child.

The personality my sister had carefully curated, born during her anorexia, was a cultured and sophisticated one filled with opera, poetry, classical music, and literature. It further cemented her place as golden girl of the family and she knew it. Now, though, she was embarking on yet another transformation. Turning her back on the earlier high-brow life, now the only people and things that appealed to her were those she had always considered beneath her. Now she let everything in, unedited. She praised and celebrated her friend Dale, a single mother with four children, each by a different father, proudly supporting her family on welfare. Grilled cheese sandwiches. "Becky, I have discovered grilled cheese sandwiches! They are wonderful!" All of it was odd and so unlike the Nancy that we all knew. And Zen. She began making pilgrimages to Zen retreats, spending days at a time in meditation. "You have no idea how hard it is to sit in a pose for eight hours a day," she told me.

"Why, then, do you do it?" is the question I never asked.

Returning to college after my winter break of 1974, I went to the loft to pick up a box that contained my Christmas gifts, which included a case holding a set of twenty *Rapid-o-graph* pens. These are the gold standard for ink drawings, each of a different width, and I was anticipating using them in my architectural drawing course. I looked in the box. There was a gaping hole where the pens had been. I was sick.

"Nancy, where are the pens? What happened? Was the car broken into? Why is everything here but the pens?"

"I have no idea," my still beautiful sister said, expressionless. With the unexplained disappearance of my pens, and a haunting suspicion that my sister was involved, a new image of her was emerging and it was far from perfect.

More than ten years later, while moving out of the loft, Rachel found the now very old brand-new set of pens tucked away in the back corner of a storage closet. They had never been used. My sister had taken them, I can only assume, to keep me from having them, to keep from me the one thing over which I had expressed unbridled enthusiasm and joy.

I sat at the desk in my dorm room, Hermes typewriter in front of me, trying to complete a term paper. Always ready to entertain anything that might distract me, I often looked up and out the big window overlooking the walkways of the handsome Columbia University campus. The black rotary dial phone sitting on the desk rang. I picked it up, grateful for the interruption. "I cannot find Nancy, she won't return my phone calls," my mother hysterically blurted. "Do you know where she is? Do you know anything?"

"I do not, Mom," I said. I slammed the handle of the phone back into its cradle. I had become nothing but a conduit to my sister by that time.

It was slowly dawning on me that no one, especially my family, was ever going to allow me to place myself first. That was a gift that only I could give myself. A lifelong battle, I began that day to practice placing myself first in small incremental ways. In my tiny dorm room, a mere 8 x 10 feet, I took the phone off the hook that day and kept it off for days. I would learn that I can create and control my own space, if nothing else. It may be that day that I learned that I could have an impact on my own environment. Recalling my sister's little apartment at 52 Garden Street, and my childhood beautiful bedroom, I began to understand the power I had to create my own "home," even in a tiny dorm room.

There was no place for me in the equation that had become my fractured family. My sister had always been the golden girl, the perfect, brilliant and beautiful daughter. Now she was unravelling and her behavior solidified her place — front and center — in the emotional life of the family, a place she managed to maintain until my parents' deaths. This was the final nail in the coffin of Trumbull Family Part 1. After the sudden and tragic deaths of two brothers, the painful, real, and ongoing decline of my sister over many years was infinitely more unbearable. With death there is no hope; with mental illness one can always delude oneself.

Struggling through my next exam period, I called home often. My father always answered, saying my mother was sick and couldn't come to the phone. After he picked me up at the train station, sitting slouched in the front seat of the car, I asked, casually, "How's Mom doing?"

"She's better," he said. "She wasn't sick, though. She tried to commit suicide. I didn't want to disturb you during your exams." *WHAT? It's more important to let me get through my exams than to tell me this devastating news? How does this family make decisions? Where does the judgment come from?*

"She took all the medicine she had in the house and slashed her wrists," my father said, keeping his communications to "only the facts, ma'am," as he enjoyed saying. "I went upstairs only because *All in the Family* was a repeat." *I owe my mother's life to Archie Bunker*, I thought.

Finding her in bed with enormous bandages wrapped around each wrist and looking sickly green from the stomach pumping days before, I was furious with her willingness to add yet another tragedy to the collection. "Mom, what on earth were you thinking?"

"I saw a house with one bad brick and I thought it was me so I began dismantling the house brick by brick..." she explained, as if telling me what is in the fridge for dinner. "I needed to get rid of it. Then I was walking down a tunnel with a bright light at the end. All of my children were coming towards me, even Peter and Jon."

I couldn't comfort or even touch my mother. My sister arrived the next day. Believing she had cleverly hidden her unraveling sanity from my mother, Nancy lay down next to her and rubbed her back. It became clear that my mother's suicide attempt was the only way she could get my sister's attention. It was Nancy she wanted, Nancy who had become so increasingly absent. Repulsed by my mother's frailties, her wrinkled skin, and the huge bandages on her wrists, I was even more repulsed by her insatiable need for my sister.

After graduating from college I fell in love for the first time. At the time my sister, still a highly functioning environmental attorney, was arguing a water pollution case against the U.S. government. Excited about introducing my sister to my new love, a mathematician, I accepted her invitation for an apéritif at her place on Vandam Street. Over red wine, rather than talking about the case, she dove into a long monologue about Calculus. Immensely proud that he must have been wowed by my sister's ability to speak that language, I watched in awe as she commanded the conversation with her brilliance. Leaving her place for the restaurant, he turned to me and said, "She has no idea what she is talking about."

A week later she won the case in Washington, D.C. and her career was on an upward trajectory. The news was on the front page of *The New York Times*. Her behavior, meanwhile, was becoming increasingly erratic. In the airport returning home from her victory, she attracted the attention of an air traffic controller. Randy was the first of many men with that name with whom my sister would connect over the next few years. I learned from Randy #5 that he met my sister when she was perched on the countertop of a men's room sink, legs spread wide, hoping to entice men to have sex with her. But that day, my sister called me to tell me that Randy would accompany her on the flight home; he got on the phone to ask if I would meet them at her apartment.

"HELLO-O!!" my sister shouted when she barged in. That was the first time I heard the overly loud voice that I would come to loathe. Randy left quickly.

"We need to go out and find a tri-pod!" my sister shouted. I chased her down streets of Greenwich Village on our search, one of the many endless, exhausting, and useless errands she insisted we run. We stopped at a little corner store, known by the locals as "Ken 'n Eve's," where Kenny looked me in the eye and said, "She is psychotic."

Two years after her suicide attempt, my mother turned sixty-two and became eligible for Social Security. She marched into her boss's office and announced that she was quitting. Stunned, he said, "How about if I raise your salary from $9,000 to $12,000?"

"Too little, too late," she said and walked out. She had her plans: she was going to move to Nova Scotia, garden, and write her life story, already entitled "Impatient as the Wind."

My parents retired to Nova Scotia. "A place with two seasons," my father enjoyed saying, "two months of summer and ten months of winter." But it was a new beginning for them. Years earlier, they had moved from Schenectady, their home when Peter died, to Washington, D.C. This time they moved from Washington, their home when Jon died. Retirement was, for them, a third fresh start. Third time's the charm?

Bettina in her garden

A month into their new life in the little town of Petite Rivière, pronounced by locals as "Petite Revere (à la Paul)," my mother was digging in her garden. She charmed flowers the way she charmed people — they blossomed in her presence. She told people, "I stood in the middle of my garden with my arms reaching to the sky and hollered into the cool spring air, 'This is Life!'"

And then the phone rang. It was me calling. "There is something terribly wrong with Nancy," I said. "She is out of control. One of you needs to come. I don't know what to do."

Before my mother arrived, my new love and I sat in an emergency room where we had managed to take my sister. Lured by his soft voice and quiet strength, she took many photos of him, always cutting me out of the picture. I now know he was busy calculating how to disentangle himself from this mess and from me and return to his former girlfriend. In that moment, I hated my sister. It was the first time I had fallen in love, and the romance had not had a chance to blossom before she cut off

Hospital waiting room, my shoulder

the new growth. What I didn't know then and can only see now: my part in this romantic drama was the one of the young woman, pining away, begging to be number one, the real girlfriend. But, as it had been my whole life, second place was the only place I really knew.

The doctor spoke quietly. "She is bipolar," he said, "and she is having a psychotic episode." Naming the nightmare did not change how I was to deal with it. There were no instructions.

"We will admit her but I cannot guarantee how long we can keep her," the doctor said.

She was released the next day.

In the 1980s, mental health laws were designed to protect an individual from hospitalization against his or her will. Good mental health treatment was sparse, and the laws protected the rights of the individual from being warehoused without good care. A worthy goal. Under the law, you could be held for up to seventy-two hours until you were given a hearing. Only then, if you were deemed a danger to yourself or others, would you be kept longer. If not, you were released. Streets were now filled with people who had at one time been given a roof over their head, if not actual treatment.

Bi-Polar illness, once called Manic-Depression, is named for the two polar opposite ends of the emotional spectrum. Mania includes periods of great excitement, euphoria, delusions, and hyperactivity. My sister was manic. I had never seen mania before and it was raw and scary. I was so lost. My mother finally arrived.

Paralyzed, my mother and I stood to the side, in horror, and watched as Nancy teetered on the parapet of her building, five stories above the ground, holding a butcher knife at her throat and screaming at the top of her lungs. "I am the sacrificial lamb in this family! I have to save everyone else!"

"Nancy," I said, in my most soothing — and always deep and throaty

— voice. "Nancy, you don't have to save anyone. It's OK, everything will be OK." I was not at all convinced of this.

"STOP!" she turned toward me in anger as she stood terrifyingly close to losing her balance. "You know nothing!" And she pointed the butcher knife at me.

The venom might as well have been injected into our veins. We were helpless. Then, suddenly, all was quiet, and Nancy gently stepped down. Her anger and energy momentarily depleted, she crumbled into tears and defeat. Thinking this nightmare might end, my mother and I looked at each other wondering what to do next. But the energy returned.

"YOU!" she yelled, reaching out to grab my arm. She stabbed her lit cigarette into my flesh, over and over. By then I was trapped underneath a stairway and there was no way to escape. I was powerless to counteract her strength and break her grip. Thinking my life was about to end, the smell of burning hair and sharp pain of each new burn hardly registered.

My mother stood nearby, watching in horror, crying, "Nancy, stop! Please stop! Rebecca has not done anything — stop! Stop!" Not only did she not stop, she then turned towards my mother and unleashed her pent-up anger at my mother.

"Shut up, Mom. You never knew how to be a mother! And you — " She put her face inches from mine. "You have made it impossible for me to be a good mother to Rachel. You have ruined it for me!"

She stepped back, holding the knife out like a sword. "There are no real men in our family — they all shrink and collapse in on themselves when we need them to be men. They cower, they cringe. Daddy has never been a man."

My mother, resisting the opportunity she was given to agree with Nancy, said, "You're tired, we're all tired. Let's lie down and get some rest."

In contrast to the mood-lighting offered by candles, my sister's preferred approach, movie-strength bright lights stayed on all through the night, night after night. Loud music filled every square inch of space in the apartment, day and night. We simply watched as my sister went about life at breakneck speed for hours upon hours, day after day. It took her about an hour to paint the walls of her bathroom a bright teal blue, not a color she might have chosen in her more subdued days. She stood at the sink in her kitchen, singing, loudly, "This land is your land, this land is my land…" And then, "Bob Dylan doesn't have a clue about how the times they are a changin.' It's bigger than he knows. I am Heloise to his Abelard. I'm going to visit Emily Dickinson in her house. She lives around the corner, you know. On Bleecker Street. No! I'm going to the New Yorker to deliver my manuscript. Capture. HL Mencken. Poetry. Who wrote Shakespeare's stuff anyway?" She rambled nonstop, often spouting strings of nonsense words in a thunderously loud voice. She exhibited an energy that was simply not human. She drank bottle after bottle of wine, straight from the bottle. This went on for days.

Years later, when describing an earthquake I had experienced, we counted out the number of seconds — a total of fifteen — and commiserated about how long fifteen seconds can be. My sister's first and scariest psychosis was our own private earthquake, and we had long ago lost count of the terrifying seconds, the hours, the days. And eventually, the years.

My mother and I finally called the police. Nancy collapsed in tears when she gave in to the straitjacket; you'd have thought they wrapped a shawl around her shoulders the way she fell into the arms of the two police officers. Maybe they were "real men."

We arrived at a private psychiatric hospital where a bearded and kind doctor greeted my sister and said, "You look as if you've been carrying the weight of the world on your shoulders." She acquiesced. That was the first time she entered an institution for what would be a long stay. It would not be the last but it would always be the best. We left her there with a sense of hope.

Recalling the question I had asked, rhetorically — I had thought — in 1972, "Which one of us will it be in 1982?" I noted that my sister, perhaps anticipating the ten-year anniversary of Jon's death, wanted to get a head start. Her first psychotic break came a couple years ahead of the tenth anniversary of Jon's death. She erupted, she proudly announced, on the same day as the volcano at Mount St. Helen's in 1980.

The head of the hospital called me that evening and said, "We will do our best to treat your sister. But you need to know that a person with manic depression often does not accept treatment. This illness can often be harder on the family than on the patient herself."

Years later, after I had celebrated my fiftieth birthday with my husband and children, the phone rang at three thirty in the morning.

"Hello?" I said.

"Rebecca! I have just bought a beautiful farm here in Nova Scotia! Joe and I are going to move there when he gets out of jail — "

"Nancy, stop. It's the middle of the night and I have to go to work in the morning. I don't want to hear about your farm now."

"But Rebecca, it is wonderful — south of Broad Cove, with a little house that is falling down — and it's ours — Joe's and mine!"

"Nancy, stop! Call me when you've come down from this high. You can tell me then about the farm. And about Joe. But don't call me in the middle of the night." I hung up.

My husband turned over and muttered something.

"It's nothing," I said. "Just Nancy."

My sister had not bought a house in Nova Scotia. By then my sister had suffered from manic depression for more than twenty years. She was delusional as she had been so many times before. She had

Nancy and Joe

Little As You Were

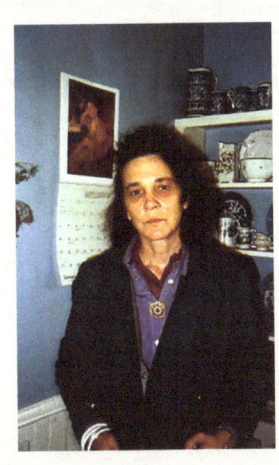

Nancy, Nova Scotia

long since finished with the men named Randy and moved on to numerous other men. She had met a fellow named Joe, a hoodlum who spent more time in jail than out. When out of jail, he beat her, like so many had before him. My parents continued to believe, throughout the roller coaster ride of my sister's mental illness, that if she would just breathe the fresh air of Nova Scotia, she would magically get better. She went to Nova Scotia and instead met Joe and together they raided my parents' house. They stole jewelry and forged checks, emptying out my parents' bank account. My sister ceremoniously threw away everything related to me, including the life-size batik I had made of the Archangel Michael that hung in the barn. A double frame with my sister's and my wedding photos once sat on my mother's dresser. My sister tore the frame in two and threw away the side with my photo. She left the portion, clearly ripped away from its other half, with her own wedding photo, the photo I had once proudly displayed on my dresser in my newly finished bedroom.

Her vitriol towards me was undeniable by then and yet my parents continued to ask me to love her in spite of it. My love, the message was, would save her. It reminds me of the burden placed on me by my father when I confronted him about his alcoholism. I became the critical element that would make others' lives better. I had the power to save everyone, my parents believed. Like many years earlier when I thought it was my responsibility to make my mother happy, I now was the linchpin in my sister's happiness. My parents forgave my sister, endlessly, for her behavior towards me, and begged me, above all else, to love my sister.

Nancy's voyage, her twists and turns, drove the emotional life of all the remaining family members. She traveled up and down the East Coast, as far north as Canada and as far south as Virginia, touching upon almost every state mental hospital and jail along the way. Convinced she was smarter than all doctors, she resisted treatment. She hid medicine underneath her tongue until she could spit it out.

My sister the lawyer was brilliant at playing the game. For years she mastered the art of the hearings. She nailed every one. It was always determined that she was not a danger to herself or others and she was always released. Early on, when she was still very sharp about legal matters, my sister became the underdogs' lawyer, offering her fellow patients the legal representation they needed. She offered these services as a patient at St. Elizabeth's Hospital in Washington, D.C., the same hospital where Ezra Pound had once been a patient. Calling my parents one evening, the head of the hospital told them, "We can no longer keep Nancy. She has effectively represented each of our patients and single-handedly drained the hospital of its clientele."

The manias were very public and exhausting. While manic, she called everyone, incessantly, day and night, and showed up at our doorsteps, filthy and bedraggled. The depressions, private and quiet, were equally exhausting. Depressed, she simply disappeared off the face the earth. The depressions were without topography, flat, with nothing there but a body breathing in tones of gray against the sound of silence. Mania. Depression. Mania. Depression. We were all exhausted. During the slide down into depression, we allowed ourselves to enjoy the brief moment when she seemed like the Nancy we remembered. *Ah*, my parents deluded themselves, *maybe this time will be different*. But we knew what was coming, and it always came. The nothingness, the absolute lack of anything but breathing. My father once arrived in Hoboken and found my sister, unconscious, in her own filth and excrement, on a bare mattress on the floor, not having had anything to eat or drink for days. Still the golden girl, though, my father called the ambulance. After each debilitating depressive episode, my parents, in their inimitable denial, believed that my sister would seek the help she desperately needed.

In time, untold drugs pharmaceutically lobotomized her and electric shock treatments killed any remaining semblance of intellect. My sister, the Harvard summa cum laude graduate, eventually managed to master the art of pushing a shopping cart to collect tin cans for change.

I hadn't seen my sister in years when Eric called. "We visited Nancy. She looks awful. She's what, sixty-six? She looks like she's ninety," he said. No one in the family was aware that she had been self-treating the pancreatic, bone, liver, and lung cancers that were devouring her body. Perhaps she was grateful that something was finally going to end her life.

 As she lay dying on a hospital bed, I was reminded of the beauty of my sister's toes, once so pretty on the family's golden girl. Her shriveled body was wracked with pain. Translucent skin appeared draped over her skeletal bones, highlighting the tendons and ligaments. Her eyes, glazed over, shifted back and forth. Unbearable guttural moans of pain filled the room if the sheet touched her legs. She cried out, "Mammie," a name she had never before in her life used. Not lost on me was that this was the only one remaining of the children my parents had, for one brief shining moment, considered perfect. From time to time Nancy caught my eye as I focused on her. During one of those moments, the loathing I felt for her for all those years fell away and I remembered 52 Garden Street, and all she meant to me as a little girl, and I said, "Nancy, I love you." Mostly I was grateful her life would be over.

 As she lay dying, it was her feet that stood at attention, with her still handsome toes pointing upwards.

7. Two Kids, Six Summers, One Island.

My sister's daughter Rachel and I lived alone on an island off the coast of Nova Scotia for six summers. This began when Rachel was seven and I, eighteen. We were joined by Woe, Rachel's yellow lab. The house had no running water and no telephone. The outhouse my father built and christened the *Richard M. Nixon Memorial* was a good distance and downwind of the house. It was wallpapered with New Yorker magazine covers.

Rachel and I were encouraged to spend our summers on the island in Nova Scotia. Our families were unravelling and on a course towards collision and no one had any room left for either of us and our needs. We were safer and happier on the island than anywhere else.

Recovering from the long trip from New York City where we lived the rest of the year, we were cozy in the kitchen, drinking tea and listening to Bob Dylan. Socked in by fog, we couldn't see ten feet out the window, and that was okay, even comforting. The woodstove kept us warm and the smell of bread baking in the oven kept us company.

"Want to read another chapter?" Rachel asked. We were reading *The Island of the Blue Dolphins* aloud to each other. That morning we had barely managed to get through the chapter in which the heroine's dog, Rontu, dies. We had sobbed through the whole thing.

I put down the quilting I'd been working on and took a sip of my tea, made with sugar and canned milk, the way Nova Scotians drink their tea.

Rachel lying on Woe

"Sure, Rach, I'll start. I think I've recovered enough." I opened the book to where we left off. Rachel lay down on the floor with her head on Woe who was curled up by the warm fire. I began reading.

I am not surprised at the trust (and responsibility) placed in (and on) us by our parents, who allowed us, two kids, to live together, alone, on an isolated island off the coast of Nova Scotia. My own childhood had come to an abrupt end when I was six and my brother Peter died, and I had taken on an adult-like role from that point on. I cannot recall a time when I didn't feel the burden of responsibility on my shoulders. And Rachel, unlike any child I have ever known, also bore the burdens of an adult way before her time; we often said she was "born old." With an unorthodox upbringing, Rachel was raised calling her parents Nancy and David; her first word, reportedly, was "Ole" in imitation of matadors at the bullfights they watched; and when she was two she accompanied the family to a concert of Janis Joplin. From age three until she was five, she spent several hours on the set of the new TV show *Sesame Street* every day, a form of day care. Way too young she learned her mother might be there for her, or she might not.

My imagined future had me, a confirmed hippie by that time, living a very quiet and simple life, perhaps in Vermont. I imagined I would wear my long hair in two braids and bake bread. The house on the island in Nova Scotia fit the bill perfectly.

As a college student in New York City, I preferred to spend time with my niece Rachel, only a subway ride away, than with my peers. Rachel, the person I loved most in the world, was the only summer companion I wanted. What might look to an outsider like a foolish and irresponsible choice on the part of both Rachel's parents and mine turned out to be one of their best parenting decisions. And so it was: Rachel and I became a twosome and lived on Hirtle's Island.

Most people would not enjoy, much less be willing to live in, such isolation. We had no plumbing and no way to connect with the outside world except for letters, which we had to boat to another island to send and receive. But Rachel and I relished it. I had spent summers tent-camping on islands; by comparison a roof over our heads and electricity felt luxurious. The fifteen-minute ride by boat from the mainland provided enough distance for us to feel a separation from the urban lives we lived the rest of the year. The water surrounding the island provided a distinct boundary around the two of us, and we felt warm and secure in the cozy little island world we created. The one concession to my teenage self? Each year I carried a collection of records to Nova Scotia. I loved my music: Bob Dylan, Joni Mitchell, Carole King, James Taylor.

Rachel, Woe and me

Nova Scotia's South Shore is a rugged and hearty coastline that faces the Atlantic Ocean. Fir trees often look scraggly and abandoned, akin to how Nova Scotians feel as residents of the Maritimes, the stepchildren of the Canadian provinces. Along this coast lies Lunenburg County, with a small cluster of islands known as the LaHave Islands. The entire area was once a bastion for fishermen and their families, because it sits in a region of the Atlantic that overflowed with fish. Fishing was a vital economy for Nova Scotia, and each fisherman, often beginning his career as a boy, "owned" a designated section of ocean for fishing; these fishing zones were handed down from generation to generation, an inheritance more valuable in Nova Scotia at one time, perhaps, than an estate in the Hamptons might be in New York. Each fisherman also owned a fishing boat, known as a Cape Islander. Our neighbor Mansfield's orange-and-green boat was named "Bernice Truman." A boat design that began in the northeast in the early twentieth century for fishing within a couple miles from shore, it has become ubiquitous throughout Maine and Nova Scotia. The body is usually painted a bright color, perhaps to be easily seen in the fog, and the housing above is usually white. A collection of these boats docked together conjures up a classic image of Nova Scotia — the various brightly painted boats all awaiting their next voyage out. The fishing boats arrived most days of the week — in a parade of color, seagulls hovering overhead for the dregs thrown overboard — to what was known as the "gov wharf" on a nearby island, which served as the depository for the fish caught that day. Once boats were unloaded at the wharf, the fish plant workers stood in an assembly line and picked up each fish, holding it up by its eye sockets to begin descaling, removing the innards, cutting off the head, sometimes filleting (pronounced FILL–it-ing) and getting it ready for market. Fishing was a booming enterprise and it was the thriving fishermen's families who lived on the LaHave islands.

    Hirtle's Island was named for the family of our neighbor Mansfield. Across the way was Covey's Island, named, no doubt, after a family that once lived there. The locals always referred to these islands in the possessive.

Winding your way through the islands, you might go through narrow passages of water like Wolfe Gut, Bakers Gut, and Sloop Cove, and perhaps see the Thrum Caps, rocks jutting high out of the water. If you travel the major thoroughfare between our island and Covey's, a deep channel of water known as the "Folly," you might look up and see our little barn-red house with the crisp white trim peeking out from the gray.

The House on Hirtle Island

Our house on Hirtle's Island is one of only four on the entire island. The house, by the time my parents bought it, had been abandoned for years. Its walls were still covered in the original wallpaper, now peeling, that had been plastered on top of lath, small strips of lumber that sufficed as the wall surface. Known as a "Lunenburg house," it is a classic Cape Cod with a steep, shingled gable roof. The central front door, never used, opened into a tiny entryway that led to a steep stair to the second floor, where two bedrooms were tucked within the sloped ceilings. The first-floor rooms were once used as kitchen and pantry, dining room, and parlor. The only distinguishing feature of the parlor was a fake mantelpiece that was never meant to grace the top of a fireplace. No one ever used the formal parlor in the way it was intended, mainly because the only people who ever came to visit were the families of the fishermen who lived on neighboring islands or in the other houses on Hirtle's Island. Visitors entered through the kitchen door, the real front door to a house, and sat in the kitchen, around the warmth of the woodstove, perhaps on the requisite rocking chair or maybe at the kitchen table, which is where most, if not all, socializing still takes place in Nova Scotia.

Perfect stove

The old house had no foundation, causing it to heave through frozen Canadian winters and giving its floor a topography that varied with the year and with the season. Rachel and I, accustomed to unstable foundations, bet on the solidity of the new room added to the house to replace one that had fallen down, the kitchen. We ventured into other parts of the house from time to time, mainly to sleep.

Although the new kitchen walls were never sheet-rocked and it still appeared unfinished, this room was the beating heart of the little house on the island. There was no running water and no sink, and the only stove — and oven — was a wood-burning one. This black iron woodstove, crafted at the nearby Lunenburg Foundry, was aptly named The Perfect.

Our lives were far from perfect. Just a few years earlier Rachel and I had experienced the suicide of my brother Jonathan. By not leaving a note, he left us with a glimmer of hope that it was an accident. The police report declared it a suicide, causing my mother to go to that depth of sorrow, that guilt beyond all guilt. David pulled strings, saying, "It would be of tremendous help to the Trumbull family," and the death certificate was changed to "accidental death." This made the Trumbull family $20,000 wealthier, proceeds from Jon's life insurance policy.

The more important gift the "accidental death" designation provided was to my mother, who could hold her head high publicly. She could write to her mother-in-law, matriarch of the pious and perfect Trumbull family, and say "The death was ruled accidental. Poor Jon, he had so many dreams. He was so full of life. His awkward stance must have had him trying to open the window in the middle of a warm night."

National Life sent a representative to deliver the check to my parents. A tall man, he scrunched his body into the captain's chair in the screened porch. "I am sorry about the loss of your son," he said.

"He had a new job and had just gotten a promotion and all his dreams and his whole life ahead of him," my mother said.

"But Bet, we all know he jumped," said my father. That old moral fiber, again.

"Van, that's not what the police said. He didn't leave a note."

Twenty thousand dollars did not make up for my mother's inability to find any joy in anything after Jon's death, which came ten years after Peter's. It didn't make up for my father's worsening alcoholism, which further eviscerated the family. It didn't make up for my sister's inability to get out of bed for weeks and her tortuous ongoing decline. It didn't make up for having to confirm my impression, at sixteen, that I was really on my own now.

My parents thoughtfully distributed one half of the total life insurance money to the three remaining siblings. My brother Eric used his $3,333 to buy a Gremlin, a lousy car and voted one of the 50 ugliest cars ever designed. My sister, I suspect, contributed hers towards the renovation of the loft in New York City. I eventually used mine for graduate school tuition. The remaining ten thousand dollars allowed my mother to fulfill a long-held dream of having a summer house in Nova Scotia, even though she had only two weeks of vacation each year. Responding to an ad in the *Atlantic* magazine offering a spit of land with a house on it, my mother and I took off for Nova Scotia, one of many trips she and I took together, alone, in an escape from the burden of other family members. These trips took on a life of their own. During these times we rescued as much of a relationship as was possible by then, a relationship built on shared dreams. A local fisherman showed us the dilapidated house on Hirtle's island, almost invisible from the water because of the overgrown foliage.

Beginning negotiations, my mother aimed to get them down from the asking price of $4,675. Sitting around the kitchen table one afternoon, eagerly watching my mother enjoy something for perhaps the first time since Jon died, we listened as she, empowered and fortified, called the sellers. "I'll offer $2,500," she said. This was followed by nervous silence. Then my mother said "OK."

My mother paid the full asking price of $4,675 (Canadian) for the little, falling-down house. Just getting to Hirtle's Island required two days of travel and an overnight ferry ride from Portland, Maine across the Bay of Fundy. It was about as remote as a place could be.

Eventually seeing the house for the first time, my father, not quite understanding the appeal of this little house — nor did he ever understand my mother or her dreams for that matter — harped, "Bet, this house has one good shingle and you'll rebuild an entirely new house around the one good shingle!" My sister Nancy, who always saw the world with a poet's eye, spotted a purple lilac amongst the overgrown foliage in front of the house. "But Daddy! It has a purple lilac!"

Rachel's and my days were filled with endless letter-writing, all in longhand, sitting at the kitchen table. We read, quilted, played card and word games. We picked wild raspberries and strawberries. When the lighting was right, I used Jon's Minolta camera to take photos of Rachel, whom I thought the most beautiful child who ever lived. We learned the words to many songs and sang them, often. We baked a lot. If it wasn't a raspberry pie, it was the brown bread — made with oatmeal

Rachel

and molasses, forever referred to as "Maudie's bread," for the wife of the fisherman who gave us the recipe — whose smell often filled the room. Or we baked cookies. We baked because we enjoyed it, because we could, and because the stove, always fed and warm, seemed to call out to us on those long days. Nova Scotia's high latitude offers summer days in which the daylight breaks well before five in the morning and dusk sets in after nine at night, providing long, sanguine light-filled days. The same latitude also guarantees a chill in the air most days, one made more distinct by an island location with the ocean winds and fog. Most Nova Scotia homes have a wood stove, which is fed wood all summer and cries out for someone to bake something. Rachel and I also baked because, during those six summers, we had time. On that little island is where we had all the time in the world.

While we had nothing but time, we needed it to do the hard work of living. Water came from a well behind the house and required many trips a day: first lifting the heavy well cover; then dipping the bucket, attached to a long rope, deep into the well and pulling it up, laden with fresh water, and then pouring it into a second bucket to haul back into the house. A full bucket weighed almost half as much as Rachel. Washing dishes required us to heat water in pans on the woodstove and use basins for washing and rinsing. We then had to carry the bins of dirty water outside and empty them far from the house.

Rachel was my equal companion in every way. She was much smarter than me and compensated for the many years in age difference with her intelligence. On our trip to Hirtle's Island, we always stopped to visit Bill Murphy and his family at their Nova Scotia summer house *Isabella,* the same house where Bill had taken my brother and me after Peter died many years before. On one of those visits, when Rachel was seven, we watched as Bill did his "penny trick," in which he pretended to run a penny inside his arm and pull it out the other side with exaggerated gulps in the throat. I had been mesmerized and stumped by this trick of his for years. She got it the first time.

Her extensive vocabulary, even at the age of seven, made us great partners at our favorite word game, *My Word!* The game requires a piece of paper and a pencil with which you draw a graph. And it requires thinking of a great, tricky word: words with duplicate letters and/or few vowels are good. The game consists of trying to uncover your opponent's six-or seven-letter word by guessing words with carefully chosen letters in selected spots. Your score is based on the number of letters in the other's word, and you receive extra points if you locate the letter correctly. Eventually a player gets enough letters, and some even in the right location, to uncover the opponent's word. We had long ago given up keeping track of who won or lost because it didn't matter — we played as many rounds as we needed. The joy was in discovering the other's word.

"Arbor," Rachel called out, "A-R-B-O-R."

"One hundred and twenty-five," I responded. Then, for my turn: "Cache. C-A-C-H-E."

"Zero," she stated.

"Ooooo, wonderful." Zero was a great score because it allowed you to eliminate several letters.

Our biggest daily struggle was with mosquitoes. They thrive in damp foggy air, especially when there is little wind.

One afternoon I heard Rachel mumbling as she sat hunched over her legs.

"Fifty, fifty-one, fifty-two. Argh! Rebecca, why do I get so many mosquito bites? Why do they all flock to me?"

"I don't know, maybe you smell better than me. Should we be better about bug spray?"

"And how come Van doesn't get them at all?!"

"I don't know, Rach. Maybe his old grandfather skin is so tough they can't stick their stickers in."

"Or maybe he's just stoic."

"Well, that he is, I'll give ya that. Rach, did you know that if you squeeze the sticker of the mosquito between two fingers and hold on tight, it'll get trapped and fill up with blood and then explode?"

"Really? Let's try it!" We did. The mosquito, swelled with blood, flew away, and I had a big old itchy mosquito bite on my arm.

Rachel and I saved our military might for the battle with the mosquitoes that took place each night when we got into bed. Our rooms were right next to each other and there was no door between them. I kept my bedside lamp turned on and listened for the detested buzzing sound. My hand rested on the large paperback book I attempted to read but mostly served as my weapon. I listened as the mosquitoes buzzed around my ear. SLAM!! I'd slap the paperback against the wall where the mosquito had landed. Success! A bloody carcass on the wall to add to the collection. The same sounds came out of Rachel's room where she was going through the same nightly ritual. From a distance one might have thought the bloody stains on the wall were a wallpaper pattern. Our superhero approach to the mosquitoes would fail, however, to put us in good stead for the battles we were to face in the future.

Rachel recalls our time on the island, saying, "We had conversations, lots and lots of them. That's almost all we did. We didn't have TV, or Internet. I didn't have playmates. You didn't have playmates. We had each other. So we talked about everything. The pimple on your nose. The mole on your back. The freckle on my arm. Whether you should cut your hair. Whether or not I was going to lose a tooth. What the tooth fairy might leave. Why people believed in Santa Claus. Why people believed in God. Why there was clearly no God. How seagulls sounded like old, cackling ladies. Why sea urchins broke so symmetrically, almost mathematically. Why small rocks could float. We talked about our daily lives, the weather."

Rachel and I were never alone all summer. Our most frequent visitor was Mansfield, who lived in the only house within shouting distance of us. Many afternoons, after his mid-day meal and a nap, Mansfield marched over, swinging his arms and singing loudly to announce his arrival, probably to give us a chance to run and put on clothes if need be. Before we knew it, he'd be seated in the rocker by the woodstove and opining on the troubles facing the fishing industry.

"Girls!" he said one day. "What kinda trouble you in? How come ya don't come down and help me mend my nets?" He then started in on his usual tirade about the life of a fisherman. "Dos' seas were high dis morning. I wasn't sure I'd make it back in today. High seas and 'tick' fog, a bad combination. And dos' damn trawlers — they scrape up everything off the ocean floor includin' all the young fish not ready yet for catchin' — they're killin' all the fish. Nobody's gettin' any fish. Dos' trawlers are spillin' over into our fishin' territory. It

Rachel and me

ain't fair. I don't know what we'll do. Lookin' forward to lobster season, maybe I'll make some money then."

"Oh Mac," Eula, his wife, who had by now joined us, said, throwing her head back and laughing at the love of her life. "I think it'll be a good year for lobster."

Mansfield realized he had not teased us for a few minutes. "What are you girls doin' wid all dem books? Dat's nuttin' but nonsense. You don't need dem books to make you smart. Come with me. I'll teach ya how to do somepin' useful."

Mansfield had grown up on the island and started fishing when he was ten. He could not read or write, except for signing his name. That morning, like every other day of the week but Sunday, Mansfield had headed out before the sun rose. After his stop at the gov wharf to drop off his fish and get paid, he headed home for his mid-day "dinner," the main meal of his day, with Eula.

He often brought us fish — mackerel, cod and sometimes even halibut — and this day was no exception. He brought us a whole haddock, a beautiful white fish. But I did not know what to do with a whole fish. "That'll teach you to stop readin' dem books and learn how to do somepin' useful," he said.

The summer was always dotted with family visits as well. My parents came for two weeks, their allotted vacation time. Nancy came most years. Rachel's father, David, came the first summer but his rapidly disintegrating marriage ended his visits. Every summer held a Trumbull/Murphy reunion, either at our place on the island or at their house a few hours away. These events provided a crescendo to the summer — we built up to them, Rachel and I planning and anticipating — after which things wound down again. While visits disrupted the rhythm we had established, we enjoyed having company and appreciated the extra hands to carry out the work of island living. We welcomed more players for a game of cards and more people to share in the evenings of reading aloud.

We did not have to explicitly instruct anyone to fall into line with the home we had created. My parents got the message and happily joined in. I think they were grateful that someone else was choreographing life for them. My father didn't keep a fifth of vodka stashed away, and they refrained from their daily arguments, even seeming, to get along.

My father's idiosyncracies, however, accompanied him when he arrived in Nova Scotia, including his self-righteous stubbornness. One year, after having experienced the delight of eating my Aunt Nancy's fresh fern fronds, my father insisted he was going out to "stalk the wild fern fronds" in search of a contribution for dinner. He traipsed around the island and brought back handfuls of fern fronds which he then cleaned and steamed, just the way my Aunt Nancy had done at the farm. After the first bite, the rest of us, choking and gagging on the horribly bitter vegetable, left the remaining serving on the plate. But not my father. He insisted on eating his full helping. We learned later there is only one type of fern frond suitable for eating, and it wasn't the type my father had carefully harvested and insisted was delicious.

One beautiful crisp day, my parents, Rachel, Eula and I headed out in our little motorboat on an adventure. Cape La Have Island, the largest of the islands and the one most exposed to open ocean, had always intrigued us. On a whim we took off in our boat, not telling anyone where we were going. We put-putted in our little aluminum row boat with the motor on the back for what seemed like hours. The scenery was spectacular. A blue sky, bright sun, the deserted white sand beaches of the islands as we rode by them. Hugging the shore along the way, we finally reached open ocean. Not only was the ocean air saltier, the water was much rougher than our little boat could be expected to handle. Our boat, fine in the calm and protected waters among the islands, suddenly seemed far too small and inadequate for serious ocean waves. Rounding the tip of the butterfly's wing, brutally exposed and beaten by the wind and weather, we attempted to pull into shore for a picnic. The wind now at our back, the ocean waves helped us pick up speed and we found ourselves coming into shore with quite a force. Slam! Into the sandy beach we landed, assertively. Slam! Waves slapped up over the rear of the boat, one after another, swamping it. Stunned, we all knew to hop out of the boat quickly to lighten the load. Stepping out into the waves breaking against the beach, I said "Everyone OK?" The waves, faster and more powerful than we were, continued relentlessly, swamping both the motor and boat. Words could not express the terror that none of us would verbalize: we were afraid of spending the night there, on the cold and desolate beach, with a dead motor and no one knowing where we were. Dragging the boat to higher ground, and bailing it out, we sat down for the picnic we had brought, hoping the motor would dry out while we anxiously ate our lunch. "Mac will be furious with me. I've broken his only rule: not leaving word about where I am going," Eula cried, nervously wringing her hands.

"We just need to turn the boat around and get it facing back out to sea," my father said with conviction. We had all seen what the combination of this boat and the open sea wrought, and looking out at the horizon of endless ocean, not a one of us was willing to join him in this hare-brained scheme. Resolute and stubborn, he tried it on his own, further flooding the boat.

"Oh Va-an," my mother called out in exasperation, stretching his one syllable name into two as she often did in utter frustration with him.

These were the kinds of circumstances I had found myself in my entire life. I had to assess the situation I was in, usually with my father, and, against his wishes, take charge of the decision-making going forward. I would have loved to feel as if I could depend on someone else for wise decision-making but that had never been an option. Frequently resolving problems created by others, my solutions were never exciting or heroic, nor were they clever. They were plodding and methodical, but they were strategic and as free of risk as I could manage given the circumstances. "No, Pop," I said, "we aren't going to keep trying that.

Here's what we'll do. We need to remove the motor from the boat and we will portage across this narrow section of the island to protected water. We can take turns carrying the motor. Then we'll come back and together we'll carry the boat across and remount the motor. Let's hope the motor isn't damaged by too much

Cape LaHave adventure, out of danger

water. There are enough of us, we can do this. If it turns out the motor is dead, we can row the boat home after we get to calmer waters." The sun was high and the sky clear, which meant we had a good amount of time to work. My conservative approach was our best chance, even if it might take twice as long as my father's more exciting course of action, which had us trying to get back out into open ocean. We stopped somewhere half way across the island and because we now felt out of danger, I took a photo of them, on the edge of the boat, looking towards the quieter waters.

Looking back on our summers on the island, Rachel's and my exposure to risk was greatly increased when my father was around. For someone who was so smart, as my mother often tried to convince me, my father's stupidity infuriated me. In spite of all the knowledge he gained in his years as a Boy Scout Leader, he seldom applied it to his own family.

    Rachel and I were much safer alone on the island than we were with my father around; alone, I kept us out of harm's way.

"You headin' in to the airport tomorrow to pick up Nancy?" Mansfield asked one afternoon.

"Yep," I said, " I hear there is a nor'easter coming and I am hoping it'll hold off a bit." Bad weather made any trip off the island nearly impossible.

The next morning, amidst mild fog, Rachel and I donned our checked flannel shirts and high black waterproof boots, standard fare for fisherman, and by that time, for us. We walked the beaten path alongside the wild raspberry bushes and rosebushes to the boat that we had hauled up on the little rocky beach days before. Fog had created a pool of water in the bottom of the boat. I grabbed the handcrafted Javex bottle bailer and emptied her out. Together we dragged the boat down to the water, grateful for the high tide that made the distance shorter. It was a heavy boat, but we did not question its weight. We felt powerful and capable, the two of us. Once the stern of the boat was afloat, I jumped in, headed to the rear and started the motor with a yank or two of the chain. With the motor going, I inched the boat off the solid ground and shouted to Rachel, "Hop in!" She gave the boat one last push and stepped in the bow. By that summer I had learned every inch of the shoreline and the rocks nearby and commanded the boat as if I'd been born to it. After the fifteen-minute boat ride, we landed at the beach where we replayed the entire sequence of events in reverse. Rachel hopped out and into the shallow water, the tall black fisherman's boots protecting her feet. She gave a tug on the boat, I hauled up the motor, and joined her, hopping out of the boat. "OK, Rach, one, two, three — PULL! One, two, three — PULL!" Over and over we'd inch the boat up on the shore,

Rachel in Nova Scotia garb

gradually getting it high enough to safely beach it until we returned. That day, like all the others, Rachel never uttered a word of complaint.

We had been looking forward to Nancy's arrival. On the ride home from the airport we shared upsetting news with her. "Parks Canada," I said, "is planning to take over some of the neighboring islands for public parkland and the local fishermen are planning a demonstration."

Rachel and I knew our perfect summers on the island would end if this happened. Imagining bridges connecting our island to the mainland, we dreaded the influx of people and traffic. Even today I have a recurring dream in which bridges and roads lead out to a developed Hirtle's Island. At the time, Rachel and I didn't care a bit about the people of Canada deserving access to this paradise. We may have couched our concern as one for the fishermen and the risk to their livelihood but really we had a single goal: we wanted to protect our summers.

With the looming threat, the local fisherman and families mobilized. We were going to save the fishing economy of Nova Scotia! Save the islands for the working economy it provided, not for tourism. We felt empowered, emboldened.

One beautiful early morning in July we took off in the *Bernice Truman*, with Mansfield driving, and his wife Eula, children Blake and Catherine, and Nancy, Rachel and me as passengers. We joined hundreds of other similar boats, in their bright colors, parading up the

Parks Canada protest

LaHave River, the river whose mouth feeds into the ocean and gives the islands their name. Large signs attached to the radar posts on the boats flew in the wind, "Parks Canada, Don't take Our Livelihood!" "We Just Want to Fish!" and "NO to Parks Canada!" The destination was Bridgewater, a small town — but the biggest anywhere around — with a weekly newspaper called the *Bridgewater Bulletin*. It was the kind of newspaper that indicated who had visited whom for tea on Sunday afternoon and whose cousins had come in from Ottawa for a visit. One time it reported that Ringo Starr had visited Liverpool, Nova Scotia (considered by Nova Scotians to be the real Liverpool).

The Bulletin's reporters covered the demonstration with beautiful photos of the colorful boats surrounded by seagulls above (attracted by the fish bits the fishermen threw into the water). At the end of the glorious day we retraced our route heading back out to the islands. The Bernice Truman carried us home, exhausted. Months later we learned that Parks Canada dropped their plan, in part because of our demonstration. Rachel and I were convinced we had successfully managed to save our summers. And, of course, the fishing economy.

Bath day followed the day spent in a fishing boat. I pulled out the big metal tub and placed it in the middle of the kitchen floor on the braided rug my mother had made. We filled every available pot with water and heated them on the stove, pouring newly hot water into the tub trying to keep ahead of the constantly cooling water. It was necessary to do our bathing early in the day — and quickly — as we were completely exposed in all our nakedness.

Rachel, bathtime

Wrapped in a towel, Rachel burst forth in song. "The sun'll come out tomorrow . . ." she began singing from our favorite musical Annie.

I joined in. "Bet your bottom dollar that tomorrow…there'll be sun."

Together we belted out, "Just thinking about tomorrow…clears away the cobwebs and the sorrow till there's none..." We put our arms around each other and swayed back and forth, singing about tomorrow.

Nancy tried to join in, she wanted to join in, she tried to sing along. But she could not. She didn't know the words. She sat down on the rocker and I felt her glowering look directed at me, almost through me. She could not have broken my bond with Rachel if she'd tried; it was impenetrable. She also didn't know how to stoop to the level of things that Rachel and I found fun. Nancy imagined she could be that person, but she wasn't and she never would be. She sat in the rocker, rocking maniacally, her eyes focused intently on me, watching and studying me as if I were from a different planet, oozing jealousy about how, it seemed to her, things came so easily to me. Her hands, more handsome than Georgia O'Keefe's, were in perpetual motion translating into sign language the conversation around her, a nervous habit of hers. She could not get comfortable with us or herself. And I could not get comfortable with her around. With my sister nearby, I felt ashamed at the level of entertainment that Rachel and I enjoyed — it was sophomoric, it was dumb, it was child-like — and I loved it.

The next day, Nancy was making lunch in the toaster oven. She left dripping burned cheese on the tray at the bottom. Insignificant compared to all the other, much larger things she had done — like leaving her husband and daughter for a plumber — burnt cheese was something over which I could confront my sister. She was cleverly able to escape larger and more substantive confrontations about what she was doing. But the cheese was immediate and I confronted her.

"Nancy, goddamn it, why can't you put something underneath to catch the cheese?"

"It won't crisp the bottom the way I like it," she said. Her response captured everything I detested about my sister. Her selfishness was on display: she got the cheese melted to perfection and didn't give a second thought to the person who had to clean it up. I hated her for leaving me to clean up the melting cheese, but I despised her even more for feeling as if I needed to clean up after her life. While I became more and more — my sister less and less — responsible, she continued to hold the affection of my parents in a way that I simply could not fathom.

Every summer I thought it would be different, and I would start out imagining loving my sister again. But as the summers went by, I anticipated her visits less and less and suffered them more and more. Tension clung to her like the dirt that surrounds the cartoon character Pig-Pen. I could not wait for her to leave. We did not know then that she was staving off her final decline into mental illness.

For Rachel and me, the soul of our summers was in the surrounding weeks when we were there alone, just the two of us. We never seemed to tire of those days.

The days were endless and full. We read a lot of books. When, years later, I asked Rachel what she remembered, she recalled, "The first thing I remember is talking about *Jane Eyre*. You had a huge influence on my taste. We talked about, and therefore from you I learned to love, Lauren Bacall. Paper Moon. Feminism. And, of course, we talked about music! We listened to and talked about Dylan, Joni Mitchell, Joan Baez, the Beatles, the Byrds. And their lyrics led to all sorts of conversations. 'Big Yellow Taxi' led to Rachel Carson and I read *Silent Spring*. We read a lot those years. We talked about what we were reading. And we sang along. I particularly remember singing with the Byrds 'To everything, turn, turn, turn, there is a season, turn, turn turn . . .' And, of course, where oh where was Wabasha? Do you remember that? Dylan's crackling voice saying they'd meet at 56th and Wabasha? We talked about right and wrong. Ethics. Behavior.

I remember doing a lot of dishes! Or you doing a lot of dishes, and me drying a lot. I remember doing things together — baking chocolate-chip-coconut-walnut bars, hauling the boat up and down the beach, picking flowers, raspberries, wild strawberries, and playing *My Word!* I remember giving you a lot of massages. I grew up to have the same 'spot,' just under my left shoulder blade, about the size of a large walnut."

What I remember is a sense of utter contentment.

Neither of us wanted to go back to real life, to school, to the world of people, to our families, to a world that wasn't visibly surrounded by a protective body of water.

The last of the summers, when Rachel was thirteen, I was already living on the island when a friend brought her from the airport. She had just completed a three-week canoe trip in northern Canada, the first time she had ever spent a summer anywhere but with me.

I threw my arms around her. Her thin arms attempted to hug me but they failed. Thin, so painfully thin, so thin that her jaw and teeth projected the way they do on a skeleton, there was no fat to fill out her face. Cold and unsmiling, she didn't look me in the eye. Rachel wasn't there.

I stepped back, desperately reaching for an earlier time. "Rach, your bed is made, put your stuff down and come sit down with me. I have a game of *My Word!* ready for us and I have a great word!"

But Rachel went to her room and lay down on her bed. She opened a book and curled up under her heavy comforter. She was cold. I made myself a cup of tea and sat alone at the kitchen table by the Perfect woodstove.

Change had come to island life by this time. Parks Canada wasn't the threat to the fishing industry that we had all expected it to be. The threat was the one Mansfield had warned us all about — large corporate trawlers who scooped up everything from the bottom of the ocean, destroying all ocean life in its path. There were no more fish. The gov wharf had closed. A sign of the future was that Maritime Tel & Tel had by then connected the islands via telephone, and we were the proud owners of a black rotary dial phone. The day that Rachel arrived looking so worn out, so thin and pale, I answered the ringing phone, a still unfamiliar sound in the quiet of the island.

Rachel's father, who had dropped her at the airport that morning, said in his deep voice, overflowing with pride, "Doesn't she look terrific?" David desperately wanted a life different from the one he was living.

Stunned into silence, I stood for a minute watching out the window as a boat meandered through the Folly. Finally, I responded, "No, David, she doesn't look terrific, she looks terrible, she looks horribly thin and sick."

Painfully reminiscent of her mother who was anorexic at the same age, Rachel had sought an opportunity — in her case the canoe trip — to get control over her life. She began a downward spiral of weight loss that would bottom out two years later at a death-defying fifty-nine pounds. Not only was she skeletal, the Rachel who arrived at the island that day was no relation to the Rachel I had known. I could not find the person I loved. There was no laughter, no singing, no joy. A stranger had replaced my beloved niece, my companion.

Rachel had begun to do the only thing she knew to survive the disaster that became her family. She needed to gain some control of her life and she did it the only way she knew how: she stopped eating. Years earlier I had hitched my wagon to Rachel's family to escape from the alcohol-infused arguments that filled the silent spaces in my own home. Now, her family, too, was unraveling. Nancy, seeing me as a threat to the tenuous hold she had on Rachel, despised me. She envied my connection with her own daughter. By this time my sister had left her marriage and family for good, and Rachel and her father spun a cocoon around the two of them. There was no room for me anymore.

Like Rachel, I needed to gain some control over my own life, which was suffocating under the weight of my family's expectations.

I left New York. I started graduate school in Virginia, far away from any family members. I created a home for myself. Not much bigger than the tiny dorm room years earlier, I started with my one-room apartment in Charlottesville. As I studied the history of architecture and dove deep into the details of space and its impact on human beings, I began to connect my love of architecture with a love of making a home.

Rachel kept losing weight while I relished learning all the nuances of Ionic, Doric and Corinthian columns. I began to prefer buildings to people, particularly family members. As Rachel disappeared, quite literally, farther into anorexia, I crafted my own future. Unlike the years spent worrying about my brother Peter and his future after being expelled from Andover, no one worried about me and my future. No one, it seemed, had ever worried about me.

Rachel and I were each on our own paths trying to gain some control over our lives. Each of our survival mechanisms was fueled by the profound love we once had for each other and eventually the sad recognition that we now faced a future with the inability to love one another. We were both too damaged.

On the island, for those wonderful summers, Rachel and I successfully kept the unraveling of our families at arm's length and made ourselves a home. It was the nicest home I had ever lived in. It didn't include the sadness surrounding the suicide of my brother Jonathan or the death ten years before that of my brother Peter. It didn't include my father's secretive drinking to soothe his pain or my mother's depression. But we were unable to keep at bay the ugly implosion of Rachel's parents' marriage, my sister's slow and painful spiral into the madness that would consume and ultimately kill her, and the utterly devastating effects it would have on my family.

Years later, Rachel asked me, "Why did you abandon me?"

"Rach, my whole family expected me to fix everything and everyone. To solve everyone's problems and make everything right again. It was an impossible task asked of me and I could not do it."

But why did you abandon me?

"Rach, I needed to leave New York. Nancy's needs were eating me alive. I was suffocating."

But why did you abandon me?

"Rach, when you landed in the hospital I flew down from Boston, and broke the hospital rules (anorexic patients were not allowed family visitors) and found you, skeletal and shivering, in your bed. I crawled in next to you and stayed there until my flight back the next day."

But why did you abandon me?

"Rach, there was no place for me in New York anymore. I needed to begin to live my life. I tried and tried to bring you into my new life — to bring you to Virginia, to Italy. Your parents wouldn't let you come."

But why did you abandon me?

"Rach, I dreamt that one day I would be able to offer you a place in the healthy and happy family I was determined to make. When I finally had a place to offer you, you were no longer interested."

But why did you abandon me?

"Rach, I needed to save my own life."

Her question, of course, would have been better directed towards her mother than me. Only in the seventh decade of my life do I finally realize that the responsibility for Rachel's life should never have been laid at my feet, nor should that of my father's alcoholism, my sister's mental illness, or my mother's life-long misery.

The only life I managed to save was my own.

Rachel and her husband, Adam, now live on the island from May to October every year, accompanied by their yellow lab, Folly. There are still no fish in the water but I understand the lobster are plentiful. Rachel tells me that life on Hirtle's Island still involves washing a lot of dishes.

8. The Most Wonderful Doll in the World

*With the greatest respect and appreciation for Phyllis McGinley, author of the book by the same name

I didn't mean to lose track of my brother Christopher's ashes. When I was a young child, my mother asked me to scatter them together with her ashes when she died. The problem is — and I don't mean to make excuses — September 11 got in the way.

My mother and I were in her room folding laundry. I was about nine years old. My job was to match socks and fold the edge over a pair to hold them together. I sat near the large, rectangular wooden trunk she kept at the foot of her bed, which held things that were special to her. To open it, you pushed a knob to unlatch and fold back the top. There was a key as well, but my mother never used it.

My mother opened the trunk to put away a scarf and pulled out a photo of herself as a little girl with her mother and father behind her. I relished this time alone with my mother and especially going through items in her trunk.

"This was me as a little girl, Becky, and these are your grandparents, Claudia and Alvin," she said to me. "Look, Becky, this gold necklace was your grandmother's."

She held the necklace up and placed it around my neck. I felt special. She put her cheek next to mine, and together we looked in the mirror. I tipped my head first to one side and then the other, marveling at the necklace, and we smiled at each other in the mirror.

My maternal grandparents' deaths had left my mother, an only child, as the last and youngest member of the family, which consisted of only half-aunts and uncles, none of whom had children. She was outnumbered by my father's family — a bustling collection of five siblings, with a total of eighteen. They were a wonderful, lively group of people who did good deeds, like saving starving children and arguing against the use of toy guns. My mother felt suffocated by their piety; a will my mother wrote when I was young (her legal secretary training made her the author of all legal documents for the family) stated that, in the event of her death, I was not to be raised by any members of the Trumbull family. The day my mother and I looked through her trunk may have been the only time and attention we ever gave to her side of the family.

There were many special things in the trunk — family jewelry, a favorite torn sepia-toned photograph of Uncle Datus, known as Date, in a broken and tarnished silver frame, and an envelope with a lock of hair from my first haircut. As I look back on it, these were the precious items that connected her to her diminishing side of the family.

Then she pulled out a little tin can. That's when she told me about Christopher.

"He was my first baby, Becky. The doctor was called in from his round of golf to deliver him. He squeezed the forceps so hard it broke many of the baby's bones. Little Christopher couldn't survive. He died five days later."

How did she fit a little, tiny baby into this can? Did she put him in head first or feet first? Does a dead baby shrink to become that small?

"Becky," my mother said. "Someday, when I die, I want you to mix Christopher's ashes with mine."

Ah! This answers my question, she burned her baby. But then . . . What?! You burned your little baby? Those little feet with the dimples, and those tiny toes? What happened to his eyes? And when you die, you'll be burned too? And become ashes? Can't we please just have one of those big marble slabs that we see at the cemetery?

Young Bettina and Van

Learning about Christopher confirmed for me a feeling that had lingered for a long time. Now I knew that my mother had lost not only Peter but also Christopher, and she expressed greater affection for them than for me, her living, breathing child. *I am here! Look at me! Please, Mommy, I love you!* I would scream in my head, to no avail. A dead child can never disappoint again — the child is fixed in time, in space, with a love that is true and real and can never again be burdened by the messiness of life itself. Over the years I have promised myself that I would react very differently if I were ever to experience such a tragedy, but I have also begged never to be tested. In that begging — to whom, I don't know — I could feel my mother's profound loss. As a child, I always harbored great sympathy for my mother and the loss of her children. I knew that I came in second place to my other siblings, both dead and alive. It seemed almost selfish of me to want my mother to love me.

The affection my mother held for her dead children extended to other things as well. She mourned objects she had lost rather than enjoying those she had. Every time my parents moved, they had to dispose of things, and my mother always carried with her regret for items she had left behind. She constantly mourned objects no longer in her possession, children no longer alive, former loves. "That beautiful tall secretary," she'd say, or "my collection of antique dolls." Her favorite children's book, *The Most Wonderful Doll in the World*, is not really about a doll at all. It's about Dulcy, a little girl who found it hard to be "satisfied with Things As They Are" and stopped playing with any of her dolls because not one of them could compare with her exaggerated memory of the doll she had lost. Very early I learned that nothing — no living child, nothing — would ever be more important to my mother than what she had lost. And she would never be satisfied with things as they are.

Why didn't my mother ask my sister, an adult by that time, to handle the ashes? Because very little was asked of my sister. She held a very special place in my parents' hearts, as evidenced by a letter my mother wrote: "Dear Nancy, . . . you were everything that life could have wanted for both of us. . . . You were the wonderful ones, you and Pete. The poor others have had to get along with our leftover love."

Not only was little asked of my sister, I was always asked to do whatever was required to accommodate her wishes. As a new mother myself, I was asked by my parents to break the "no smoking" rule in our house to accommodate my sister's incessant cigarette smoking. At the height of Nancy's mania, spewing anger and blaming me for most everything, my mother said, "Please just love her. That will help her get better." Their own love for her had failed to help her get better, so why did they think that my love would help? Did they ever consider the burden on me when they tried to transfer this responsibility to me? If anyone considered the impact on me it was an afterthought at best.

The task regarding the ashes was beneath my sister, perched on her pedestal. As a child receiving leftover love and the second-best daughter,

I was there, in the room and in the moment, so my mother asked me. For me this was simply the way things were; it never occurred to me that this was too great a responsibility for a young child, or that I deserved anything more.

Three years earlier, when I was only six, I had assumed a much greater responsibility. It was then that Peter died, and I saw it as my role to make my mother happy. I was young enough to think I had the power to make someone else happy, but I was not old enough to know that it wasn't my responsibility. No one ever told me that it was, but no one ever told me it wasn't, and until the day she died, I carried that impossible task on my shoulders. None of my siblings ever thought to relieve me of this weighty responsibility, nor did they offer to share the load.

How did they manage to escape my mother's grief with a sense of freedom to lead their own lives, while I became burdened with the unachievable responsibility of making my mother happy? Of course, it turns out that they never really escaped anything. Their demons simmered for many years before they surfaced.

Mixing Christopher's ashes with my mother's? It would be at some point far in the future and simple by comparison, it seemed, to the more immediate and infinitely more difficult task of making my mother happy. The day I learned about Christopher was the day that I realized that a shroud was draped over my family like the heavy black velvet that lay over Peter's casket. Both Peter and Christopher's deaths were not aberrant, isolated incidents for my family; they were pieces of a much larger and longer story, one that held secrets that I would not learn for years to come. As a child, I found solace in imagining that the shroud over my family was like the thin, black, lacy veil draped over Jackie Kennedy as she walked down Pennsylvania Avenue alongside the riderless horse just a year before. A thread of sorrow wound its way through every aspect of my family. Learning about Christopher deceived me into thinking I understood the full depth of my mother's grief, and my responsibility for her happiness became exponentially more difficult.

The request made of me regarding the ashes had an upside. It made me feel important. I had so often felt insignificant, a leftover. Every holiday season my father prepared special almonds, first blanching and removing the skin, then salting and carefully roasting them, and turning them often to keep them from burning. He packaged these, tying them with ribbon, and gave them as gifts to all his female coworkers and friends. My sister was always at the top of his list. Not me: I got the leftover broken pieces on the cookie sheet. But in my new role as the caretaker of Christopher's ashes, I stood slightly taller.

Christopher was born in the 1930s, when women were put to sleep to have their babies and stayed in the hospital for weeks afterwards to recover. My mother awoke not to a suckling infant but to a dying baby. My parents had his body cremated and stored his ashes in a little tin can.

After school each day, when I left Miss Patsy's fourth grade classroom and came home to an empty house, I often went into my mother's room, tempted to look inside the trunk. One day, I got up the nerve. I took a deep breath and folded back the lid. I felt around for the tin can and finally wrapped my little palm around it. I held it, the silver-colored, crematorium-issued cylindrical can labeled "Baby Trumbull." I sat down on the bed to steady myself.

Will Christopher pop out of the can like a jack-in-the-box?

I carefully took off the top. Nothing happened. I lifted my eyes to make sure I was still alone in the room, then I looked deep inside the can, hoping to see what Christopher looked like. The house was silent. I stared at the grey-textured ashes. Having grown up with fires in a fireplace and campfires in the summer, I knew these ashes weren't like any I'd ever seen before. Slowly, and very carefully, I slipped my fingers into the can and moved my hand around. I pulled out a few big pieces; this wasn't fly-away ash, it was pieces of bone.

How do they burn a body? Do they slide it into an oven on a big wooden paddle the way a pizza is slid into an oven?

The wooden trunk followed my mother when my family moved from our home in Schenectady, New York, to Washington, DC, in 1967; it moved again to Nova Scotia, when my parents retired there in 1980, and finally to their last home. To prepare for my parents' last move, I went to Nova Scotia to help gather their favorite belongings. There was furniture — the drop-front mahogany secretary desk my mother had found at an auction in Nova Scotia; the marble-top dresser that had always housed her most prized linens; and the ladder-back chairs and drop-leaf china and her black Steinway piano. I brought the beautiful, long, black velvet dress that she had worn as a teenager, and that I, years later, wore as a teenager and imagined someday my own daughter would wear. I packed my mother's favorite paintings and, of course, her trunk.

The black velvet dress

I imagine we would have called him Chris, or maybe even Topher, but we never again talked about Christopher. Would he have had the small, pug nose and square jaw that graced the faces of my sister Nancy and my brothers? Or would he have had the sharper, beak-like nose that Jonathan got? Would he have been a writer? Or a lawyer? Would his hair have been my mother's red or, like mine, brown? When I was an adult, my mother gave me the unedited version of his death as she saw it: "That goddamned doctor just wanted to get back to his golf game. He murdered my baby."

My parents' last home would be in a retirement community in Philadelphia ("Damn it," my father would say, "Don't call me a senior citizen. I'm an old man!"). My father, paralyzed by a stroke, lived in the nursing home section so that he could be turned over by nurses each night to prevent bedsores. My mother had graduated from one level of care to the next and was now ready to join my father in his nursing home room. My husband, our two children and I had moved to the West Coast by this time, and in spite of the distance, I continued in the role of primary caretaker of my parents' lives. To help with my mother's move into my father's room, I reserved a flight from San Francisco to Philadelphia for September 18, 2001. Everything was all arranged.

The morning of September 11, 2001, my husband and I woke to the radio at six, Pacific Time, and soon heard the report of a plane crashing into the World Trade Center. In my sleepiness, and before anyone knew the magnitude of the tragedy, I recalled memories of the World Trade Center: my brother Jonathan, a newly minted assistant district attorney, so proud to be working in the building when it first opened in the 1970s; and the time I went to the restaurant — *Windows on the World* — and was loaned a pair of pants by the maître d' to replace the dungarees I was wearing.

By the time it was clear this was no accident, my husband and I were downstairs watching the television news, and the kids straggled in with their sleepy school-morning faces. I was tortured by the distance between my new and still unfamiliar West Coast life and the unfolding tragedy taking place in the city I once called home. Why was I so far away? Terrified for my fourteen-year-old son and nine-year-old daughter, I confess I took comfort in believing that terrorists would not venture to what felt to me at the time as a god-forsaken part of the country.

The kids and I stayed home. I baked all day. At dinner that night, when we all sat around the table as we did every night, I announced that I couldn't travel to the East Coast.

"Mom, good idea. Stay here with us," my son said, detecting my anxiety. I bristled at the idea of him feeling as if he needed to take care of me — something I had avoided at all costs — but I was grateful for his empathy.

"There must be another way to move your mother," my husband said, inviting me to consider that the solution did not have to include me.

I cancelled my trip. Did my children need me then? I am not sure, but I needed them, and my husband, and I needed to continue with our family rituals, like the dinner we had together each evening. I wish I could say that this national tragedy finally allowed me to pass the torch within myself, that it gave me the freedom to place my own needs and those of my own family above those of others. That process, however, is ongoing even today, and as long as a winter night. But that day it became absolutely clear to me that it was time for someone else to make my mother happy.

"Li Hua," I said when I called my parents' most wonderful caregiver. "I cannot come. Would you please move my mother in with my father?"

"Of course," she said, her answer to anything I asked of her. The day of the move, she telephoned me; between her halting English and my inability to recall the room and its contents, we did the best we could. Li Hua arranged the move of my mother's blue chair and her favorite bedside table and hung her favorite photos on the wall. She took my mother out to a Chinese restaurant to celebrate, even though there was little reason to celebrate.

The move had gone just fine without me.

A few days later, driving to work along a stretch of Masonic Street I soaked in the breathtaking view of the morning sun lighting up the city of San Francisco. As if punched in the stomach, I realized my mistake. The trunk. I had forgotten the trunk. How could I? The trunk had been a fixture for most of my life. My mother had watched over Christopher's ashes for sixty-six years by that time. I pulled over to the side of the road and replayed the events in my mind.

"Goodbye, Christopher," I said out loud. "If you had lived, Christopher, everything might have been different."

I called the manager of the retirement home where my mother had been moved, from an apartment to the room with my father in the nursing home section. Her apartment had been readied for a new occupant, I was told. The trunk — with the ashes — had been emptied into a dumpster, and all the furniture was given to others at Stapeley. The clothes in her closet, including the black velvet dress, were given to Goodwill.

By this time my mother was so old and confused that she didn't remember Christopher's ashes or the black velvet dress. I did. Even today I try to shed the thought of them and all the years I lived, knowingly and sometimes not, with my mother's longing for all that was no longer within reach.

9. Deoxyribonucleic Acid, or DNA

Bill Murphy was ninety years old when I last visited him in Nova Scotia. After dinner one night we sat together, alone, in the fireplace room.

"Rebecca," he said, and I knew it was serious by the tone of his voice and his use of my given name. Otherwise he would have called me Rebequah or Beck-a-noodle. "I have something to tell you," he said. I shifted a bit, unsettled. "Rebecca, when your family and mine met, many, many, years ago, your mother and I fell in love. We were both married, each with three young children, and we agreed not to ruin our families. But we loved each other dearly and we loved you, the child born of our love. We agreed that we could not leave our spouses but we never lost our love for one another. I have always tried to give you what I would have wanted to give you as your father — a sense of yourself as a good, strong, smart, and beautiful woman. Your mother and I always promised to keep this information from you, not wanting to complicate your life, but now I regret that we did not share this news with you when your mother was alive. She would present this information to you in the same way that I have. We loved each other and we both loved you, even if we could never acknowledge it publicly."

That conversation never happened. Here is what I do know:

My mother and her husband, Van, and their three children met Bill and his wife Tottie, and their three children sometime around 1947, through the Unitarian Church in Schenectady, New York. The perfectly matched intellectual powerhouse families became fast friends, united in their displeasure with organized religion, their love of the English language, similar politics, and simpatico senses of humor. In the early years of their friendship they spent an extraordinary amount of time together as families, although that had waned by the time I was born. They remained friends until my parents died.

I visited Bill's son Chris recently, a couple years after the last of the four parents had died. Through the years Bill had implored me, "Please always stay in touch with Chris." Sitting in the comfortable chairs in his living room, over a glass of wine, we talked.

"Noodle" he said, "did you know that your mother and my father had an affair?"

I did not. And I was shocked. Chris grew up knowing about it, he said, because as a young child he overheard his parents arguing behind what they thought were closed doors. He heard the salad bowl being flung across the kitchen, hitting the opposite wall. He heard Tottie yell at Bill, "This must stop or I will tell Van!"

"NO! Don't do that! Van would kill me!" Bill said.

"I think the affair ended sometime in 1955," Chris said. I was born in 1955.

I looked at Chris, and the scenes of the lunches with Bill, the many poems he wrote me, and the valentines he sent me every single year, signed only with a question mark, all swirled around in my mind. As it dawned on me, I said, "Do you think I could be Bill's daughter?"

With a twinkle in his eye, he raised his eyebrow as if asking me the same question. As an adult, knowing what he knew, Chris said, "Even in the most recent Trumbull/Murphy get-togethers, I watched your mother and my father share knowing glances, hoping perhaps, to steal a moment alone together. But my mother watched over them like a hawk."

While clearly my mother, Bill, and Tottie all knew, there is no evidence that my father knew anything. The Murphy children knew something was going on. I will never be able to ask my siblings from Trumbull Family Part 1 because they were all dead by the time I learned of this. My only remaining brother, Eric, did not know anything. Maybe Bill wanted me to keep in touch with Chris because he knew that he was privy to arguments about the affair and would share that information with me. He hoped that, between us, we would figure it out.

Sitting with the possibility for several weeks, I studied old photographs, noticing the now obvious resemblances between Bill and me: lack of a chin, hairy fingers, a large and white thumbnail moon on my thumb, what I call "pigeon-toed" front teeth, and identical eye color. My friend Kathy, with whom I shared the suspicion within hours of learning it, googled photos of Bill and found the same similarities. The picture was coming into focus and I began to put moments of my life against this new backdrop. The only thing missing was a definitive answer. Knowing I needed one of Bill's children to do a DNA test, I was paralyzed by fear from asking any of them. Feeling certain that Chris would prefer the romance of the unanswered question, I dredged up the nerve to ask Sue, Bill's daughter, to do a DNA test with me. I love her for her answer. Simple, quick, and definitive. "Yes. I always wondered why Dad had a special place in his heart for you."

DNA testing is not something that my parents' generation could have anticipated being so readily available. Submitting my vial of spit, I studied up on how to interpret the results once they came in. Then I waited. I began to imagine the possible results, one indicating I had no genetic connection to Bill and the other determining he was my father. I imagined both options. I admit: I began to worry that I would learn something I did not want to learn. A friend nailed my concerns on the head, asking, "How will you feel if you learn Bill isn't your father?" I knew then that I would be sorely disappointed. I would have to revisit again everything about my life that finally seemed to make sense. Throughout the wait, I tried to temper my expectations but knew what I wanted: to confirm that Bill was my father. I did my best to prepare for the other result, one that by then I would have considered bad news.

An email alerted me that my results were in. At first I stumbled with the computer and the technological know-how to read the report. But there it was: an almost 20% match of DNA indicates that Sue and I share a single parent. She and I are half-sisters. Bill was my biological father. I wish I could say that I felt a sense of loss, knowing that my father Van, the man who raised me, was not my father, but I didn't. No, I felt unadulterated (perhaps newly adulterated?) joy learning that Bill was my father. There was now a reason for the lingering hatred for and distance from my father I had felt throughout my life. I could finally allow myself to have those feelings without beating myself up for being ungrateful, for wondering why I could not connect with him. I also felt a tinge of pity for my father and thought again of the songs he sang to me as a child as I fell asleep.

But the DNA result finally explained so much to me, and it brought things into clear focus. The person who built me up over the years, gave me the only sense of self-worth that I have, was in fact my father. Telephoning my newly identified half-siblings Chris and Sue, I shared my joy; they welcomed me into the family and gave me a flask of Bill's ashes and photos of my paternal grandparents.

Since receiving the confirmation of my suspicions, I have replayed

Bill and me

my entire life, seeing it all with new eyes. I have looked back at all the family photographs over the years, I have read through all the letters Bill wrote me (which I had saved) and the letters I wrote him (which he had saved and Chris gave to me). I see things more clearly now: the lunches, the Christmas shopping trips, Bill taking my face into his hands and saying how much more beautiful I was than the last time he saw me, the comments dropped into every single letter he wrote me. "I miss you. But I always miss you and I suppose I always will while you're not with me…If Chaucer had known you what poetry he would have written." I reread all the poems he wrote me.

Once confirmed, I reached out to anyone still alive who might have known my parents, and deep into the recesses of my own soul. I hoped to find any clues whatsoever that might bring all this to light. Very little surfaced. However, I do recall that one day, late in my mother's life, I found a sealed envelope stating in her handwriting, "Do not open until my death" on the front. Defying her instructions, as she was very much alive, I opened the envelope. Inside, in her distinct left-handed handwriting, was a long letter saying that her life had been turned upside down when she met the Murphys, that she had felt and experienced things she had never before felt or experienced, that she could never go back to being the person she had been before. Did I ask my mother about this letter? No; I emailed Bill. His response, in an email grammatically correct and so unlike the very long emails he typically sent, said, "I have no idea to what she is referring." That letter of my mother's may be the only one never filed in a "letter book" and is gone forever.

My newly discovered half-sister Sue recalled an episode in the 1980s, during the depths of my sister's early periods of psychosis, when Nancy marched into the kitchen of *Isabella* and announced to Tottie and Sue, "Rebecca is Bill's daughter." No one challenged her or asked any questions. I am impressed, in an unfortunate way, that my sister, throughout her manic episodes when nothing was sacred, never divulged anything. On her death bed, looking skeletal, she looked at me and said, "You must have so many questions." I had no idea then what she meant, nor do I know today if she was referring to my mother and Bill.

Did any or all of the siblings from Trumbull Family Part 1 know about this? Was this the precipitating event that began the devastation of the Trumbull family? Is this what set in motion my sister's anorexia and her dramatically altered personality? Did this play a part in ultimately unleashing the mental illness that led to Nancy and Jonathan's decline? Did they feel like they were children of a lesser love? Were their impressive CVs an attempt to prove their value, their perfection? Were they burdened by having to cover for or collude with my parents? Did they feel the need to protect my father from this news? Was my sister indeed, as she had shouted from the rooftop, the sacrificial lamb? There is not a single shred of evidence that any of this is true and yet I think that all of it might be.

I am left only to my imagination and this is what I imagine:

My mother loved Bill, an enchanting and charming man, a man equal to her in his engaging manner, his ability to love. And Bill loved my mother, the red-haired, passionate, full of piss and vinegar woman. Their personalities were in stark contrast to that of their spouses. My mother's husband, the man I called Daddy/Dad/Pa/Pop for my entire life, was aloof and intellectual and always found a way around feelings by simply ignoring them. Bill's wife, Tottie, was as rough as an unhewn piece of lumber and cold as steel. Could it be that Van and Tottie became hard and detached in part because they both knew that their spouses were in love with each other? Or perhaps that is only my impression, one ingrained after years of feeling nothing but a chill from either of them.

I grew up thinking that all the misery in my family emanated from the deaths of my brothers, three sons to whom my mother and father gave birth. Losing even one child is unimaginable. The relentless pounding of one tragic event after another provided a reason, and perhaps even good cover, for what might have been at the very heart of the misery.

I now know that the despair in the family went much deeper and emanated from a place that only compounded the catastrophic grief of the death of three sons. Their acceptable public grieving for the loss of their children was able to camouflage a private hell of another kind. There could be no sympathy for the grief that could not be exposed.

I feel sorry for every single person affected by this, myself included, although self-pity has never been my strong point. Do I wish I had known about this while my mother and Bill were alive? Absolutely. Do I feel cheated of the truth? Yes. Would my life have been different if I had known this information while my parents were still alive? I suspect it would. I hope I might have been more sympathetic to my mother. Maybe I would not have taken the phone off the hook that day, refusing to answer another call from her. Maybe I would have hugged her when I first saw her, pale with bandaged wrists, after her suicide attempt. The joy that she and I came to find when alone together, unburdened by other family members, might have been exponentially greater if we could have shared this significant truth. Impossibly, I wish, desperately, for one more chance to sit down and confront both my mother and Bill with this new knowledge. Would my relationship with Bill have been different? I suspect so, and, indeed, the knowledge might have ruined the almost perfect, albeit inauthentic, relationship we had. I might have been angry with him, perhaps even severing our connection. Perhaps I would have made demands of him, demands that he could not meet. Instead, I asked for almost nothing of Bill and I received an overabundance in return. And I always wondered why.

Every single one of the players in this saga suffered through this either knowingly or unknowingly.

My mother, Bettina. After a lackluster marriage with an unsatisfying partner (in so many ways, all of which I eventually learned about in great detail), in which they experienced tragedy early, she went on to feel love and passion with Bill. But she stayed with the man whom she had married years earlier, who was not well suited to her fiery personality and did not know how to provide the kind of love, passion, support, and friendship she desired and needed. I cannot help but recall his letter to her, saying "You arouse in me aspirations that I know I never will, that I cannot fulfill." Together they marched on with their marriage only to face a relentless and catastrophic series of tragedies, like the fall of dominoes.

Did my mother and Bill ever want to leave their spouses and make a family together? Did they even discuss this as an option? Or were societal norms such that they would not ruin the impressive families they had each built with another partner? Clear throughout my childhood, and in fact throughout my life, was the fact that my mother despised my father. They managed to stay together maybe only because, sadly, at some point it becomes harder to take a different path.

Learning about Bill helps explain why, when at age seven I went in my mother's room that evening and asked her if I could be enough, she just started crying louder. It was not only her dead sons she was missing, it was Bill and the life that might have been. As I sat on her bed, I represented the product of a life she lived outside the rules and in secret, a life that was never really hers, a life whose ending may have coincided with my very birth. Was she guilt-ridden at having created a child who was not her husband's? Did she feel responsible that her husband had to support this child? Knowing her, I suspect she was simply furious that she was stuck in a miserable marriage and that the only evidence of the life she had wanted was me, the child born of the secret love. Given her absolute lack of faith, did she ever consider the deaths of her sons as payback by a higher power — in which she didn't believe — for her infidelity? Was it payback for her impiety? Did she look at me and see everything that had gone wrong in her life? Did she ever think that if only she had lived the more pious kind of life the Trumbull family members lived she would not have suffered so much? She was destined never to "be satisfied with things as they are" and was, in fact, dissatisfied until the day she died. When she tried to convince me that it is better to have loved and lost than never to have loved at all, I now know she was desperate to convince herself as well, and I now know why.

The burden of the family did not always weigh heavily — or at least front and center — over my mother and me. When we were alone together and unencumbered by my sister or anyone else in the family, we found a true kinship and came to thoroughly enjoy each other's company. Driving together to Nova Scotia one year, we might have been mistaken for something akin to Thelma and Louise. We were feisty, impassioned, unstoppable. Snowed in at a hotel off the turnpike in Maine one year, we met a man named Lew Hoyle in the hotel restaurant. Certain he was putting the moves on me, the younger of us, and, by virtue of that, the more beautiful, imagine my surprise when I discovered it was my mother he was after! Challenging my mother to a game of cards but lacking a deck, he set out to make one by cutting up paper. In that moment, I was able to recall the person my mother had once been. Spicy, passionate, beautiful. For years I teased her relentlessly about Lew Hoyle. It was my mother and I who discovered and bought the house in Nova

Scotia where my parents would retire, and for a year or so, she and I lived there while my father continued working in Washington, D.C. In those moments together and free of the clutter, we were the mother and daughter of whom Shakespeare wrote in the sonnet, we were the mother and daughter whose small family might have been complete if it had included Bill.

But those were fleeting moments and I understand now that my mother could not let me, the daughter she had with Bill, outshine my sister, her legitimate daughter with Van. She knew that my very birth was wrong, that I was collateral damage, and she needed to remind herself of that by telling me that I wasn't as smart, and certainly not as beautiful, as Nancy. She needed to bolster Nancy at all costs, and it simply did not matter what it cost me, the child of leftover love. She failed to see the impact that incessant pleading with me to love my sister had on me. She had to do whatever was needed to save my sister. She saw me as a lifeboat. Indeed, perhaps I was the true sacrificial lamb to be offered up. In fact, in retrospect, I was the true golden girl.

Bill, my biological father. Did he love my mother? I can only surmise based on little things dropped into letters, and his complete and utter adoration of me, that not only did he love my mother but he worshipped her in a way that translated to a worship of me, their joint effort. He must have known I was his child. There is no other reason he would have bestowed such attention upon me all those years. "I'm dying to see you Rebecca. The thought of you goes through me like a spear. How did I get along before 1955?" he wrote in a letter to me. And "I wish you and I could have a long talk soon. I'm hungry for you," from another. His granddaughter Elizabeth recently said, "it's a good thing it turns out he was your father because those are some pretty creepy things he said."

A postcard arrived one day:

Outside the Fahrenheit is 85.
Inside it's wonderful to be alive
With air conditioners and cheese and beer –
Only I wish I had Rebecca here
To talk with, walk with, watch the birds withal
Shop at the dozen markets in the Mall
Share noodle soup with; -- but for lack of these
Even a tiny lettercard would please
More than an anti-melancholic pill
Your humble and devoted servant,
    Bill

I cannot imagine that Bill suffered to the extent that others in this saga did, but he may have been hurt by the lack of greater contact with me and from the inability to shout from the rooftops that he was my father. In Bill's ten-volume memoir, where he focuses mainly on local college politics, national politics, and his own efforts at writing the Yeats' biography, he writes about our lunches together, saying, "Beginning with those lunches Rebecca and I developed a wonderful association… Her friendship over the years was one of the best things that ever happened to me." He remained true to the deception.

"Men," my mother often said, "they always get off easy."

His daughter Sue recently told me that Tottie implored in a letter sometime around the time I was born, "Your family needs you!" What led Bill to stay with his wife? Was it her tenacious grip? Had he always intended to stay with his family and never imagined leaving them? He was intensely proud of his family and dutifully (impressively and admirably, I might add) fulfilled his obligations to them. Unlike my parents, Bill and Tottie managed to have a good life, enjoying the intellectual milieu to which Bill's career gave them access.

Van, my father. His is the most confusing and profound situation. I have had the good fortune to be able to read through every single letter my father ever wrote or received during his lifetime, because he saved all the letters both he and my mother wrote and received, organized chronologically and in binders. There is not a single reference to this in any of the letters, which I had always complained were filled with bits of unimportant news and seldom any mention of the things in life that really matter. In retrospect I see how much I got that right. Was he aware that his wife loved someone else? Did he know there was a child that wasn't his? No explicit evidence exists that he was aware of this. I believe, though, that on another, much deeper level he knew about my mother and Bill, and perhaps about my parentage. He knew but hid the fact even from himself. That knowledge, which he could not and would not face, is at the heart of much of the torment in my family as I grew up. It is perhaps the reason for his anger at my mother. Early on in my marriage my father said, "The high divorce rate is not surprising to me. What is surprising is the number of people who manage to stay married." He was determined to play out his own marriage as if it had integrity. That being said, I owe him an enormous debt. If, indeed, he knew I was not his child, he did the best damn job he could raising me as if he were my father.

My father was a master of denial. He simply refused to give himself conscious access to certain information. In the height of my sister's psychosis, when she had escaped yet another mental hospital, he announced, "She's getting better, all on her own." His own son's suicide? "He got what he wanted." My family had long ago developed a well-honed approach to life: if we just don't mention something, it won't be true.

Absent explicit information about what he knew or didn't know, I am sorry for (and angry at) him for not facing his suspicion and confronting my mother. I am sorry that he went through his life thinking that someday my mother might love him again. A letter my father wrote me soon after my mother's suicide attempt, after I had pleaded with my parents to share more than the superficial parts of their lives, says "Bet doesn't love me, indeed, doesn't even like me. She's told me this many times. Vehemently. I hang onto her because I hope that even deeper underneath this is not true. I hope and hope and try to please her." This might have been the only letter among the thousands that expresses true and real emotions.

If he was the only one of the four adults who did not explicitly know the truth, was he played by the other three for the entirety of their lives, their friendship? I feel sorry for my father Van if that is the case. If true, however, maybe he shared some of the responsibility for failing to confront the issue about which he might have had an inkling of a suspicion. Given his inability to dig a little below the surface and find what he must have known was there, and if no one actively engaged him in the truth, in his well-honed approach of denial it might have been easy for him to be a pawn in the game for all those years.

It may be out of pure kindness that the other three tried to protect him. My father Van had suffered an unimaginable personal tragedy when he could not save his dying son Peter. Letters uncovered recently explore the lengths to which my father went to find an explanation for Peter's death and the myriad of possibilities he considered along the way. Early on, my father believed for several days that Peter died because his persistent artificial respiration had prevented Peter from regaining his own natural breathing rhythm. When I imagine living with that belief for even an instant the very thought makes me feel tremendous pain for my father. I have no idea where this idea came from and apparently a local physician emphatically tried to convince my father that this could not have been the cause of death. But my father lived throughout his life with the unsatisfactory cause — walking pneumonia — spelled out on the death certificate. One day, decades later when I thought it might be a safe topic, I said, "Dad, what do you think really killed Peter?"

He slammed his fist on his knee, and said, as if it had happened the day before, "Damn it, I should have massaged his heart to keep it going." Even then he was still beating himself up for not having saved Peter. CPR, which involves massaging the heart, I learned recently, had not been discovered as a life-saving measure until the early 1970s, a full decade after Peter died. That awful day at Lake George my father did everything he knew and in his power to save his son.

My father did not stand a chance. A letter he wrote my mother after a brief break up early in their courtship, says "Don't love me for my hopes and plans. Love me for my failures – or in spite of them. Alas, they are not even big failures; just little pipsqueak failures like the death of a mosquito." On top of the pile of little failures eventually came a big failure. He wasn't able to save the golden boy of the family. Even if my mother had still loved my father by that time, not being able to save Peter destroyed any hope for their future. If Peter had not died that day, would life have played out differently? Even if Van allowed himself to acknowledge the love between my mother and Bill, he was facing harsh realities: his wife did not love him; he was financially burdened by a child that was not his; and he had lost his bright shining star of a son, the adored Peter. He drank because he could not abide any of it, all of it: the loss of my mother, the loss of his children, everything.

Believing that my father probably knew about my mother and Bill, and my parentage, helps me to understand many things. Experiences with my father seem clearer to me now. He has become, in my mind, "my father, once removed." I no longer have to wonder why there was, according to my brother Eric, a delay in jumping in after me when I fell from the cliff; why I got the leftover and broken pieces of nuts he had roasted; why the rattlesnake capture was more important than my safety; why, when we motored over to the most remote part of an island off the coast of Nova Scotia, he belittled my safe and mundane approach to finding our way home, promoting his risky and dangerous method in the hope of being a hero; why he was so determined not to fill up the gas tank, such an easy thing to do, rather than trying to prove he was right, ultimately leaving me to hitchhike to the airport. He needed to remind me that I was not his daughter but rather a product of someone else, that I was a lesser being.

It helps explain why, when my father had a series of mini strokes, his speech garbled and balance non-existent, he yelled at me for suggesting a trip to the doctor, "Damn it, you don't get a say in my life!"

I now know why I could never measure up to my sister all those years, she plunging deeper into her madness and yet inexplicably held high on her pedestal by my parents, the golden girl of the family. I finally understand why I was so comfortable my whole life coming in second to someone else; it was what I had grown up with and what I knew. I now understand why my parents could not remove my sister as executrix of their will even though she could not find her way out of a paper bag by that point. She was Van's only daughter.

It explains my father's furious response when, one day, holding my young son Daniel, I commented, "Dad, look, he has your forehead!"

"Damn it," he said, pounding his fist on the table, "he has his own goddamned forehead!"

No wonder I felt the disconnect between my father and me. He was not my father. I was not his daughter.

Tottie, Bill's wife. She had a rough childhood and often shared those stories with her children. Her mother and father split up, her father committed suicide, and her mother lived with a woman in a socially unacceptable illicit relationship that, at best, excluded the little girl growing up, or might have been, at worst, abusive. She thought that in Bill she had found someone who would stand by her unequivocally. She had wanted a larger family but a requisite hysterectomy after her last birth put an end to that. Whether or not she was aware that I was Bill's child (I believe she was), she was fully aware of the relationship that very easily could have resulted in that outcome. Imagine the envy she must have felt thinking Bill had gone on to have another child with my mother, the beautiful and charming Bettina. The laser-like focus on her husband and my mother for all those years when the families got together indicates to me that she never let go of her jealousy of my mother and distrust of her own husband. I never liked Tottie. The last time I saw Bill, I asked him, "Why is Tottie so mean to me?" I do not forgive her but now I understand her better.

In the end, it might be my relationship with my family that suffered the greatest long-term repercussions as a result of all of this. In a letter Bill wrote me when I turned twenty-one, he said, "I wish I could describe to you the fullness of the visit with Bet and Van on Hirtle Island. You were the chief subject of conversation — partly, of course, because I kept talking about you, but also because Van and Bet spoke of you constantly as if you were the greatest thing that ever happened, which you are, to my way of thinking. You have become a repository for everybody's hopes, fears, gripes and bitches, mine along with everyone else's. We all depend on you."

It was that dependence on and expectations of me that ultimately became my unbearable burden.

My mother had always wished my father had one tenth of Bill's financial savvy. "Real estate is the best possible investment you can make," she implored as she watched Bill buy one house after another in Nova Scotia, expanding his "compound." This was the sort of thing my father wouldn't, or couldn't do, and something my mother desperately wanted him to do.

But when I became an adult and my husband and I focused our

efforts on our family and careers and stumbled upon a few lucky real estate investments, my mother expressed nothing but resentment towards me for my success. While she could sing my praises to others, and often did, to me she expressed only her disappointment. Hearing my father's voice many years before, "I wouldn't drink if you treated me better," the message I received was that every disenfranchised member of my family would be better if only I would have done something differently. I had not loved my sister enough to save her from her own fate. I had not bought my sister a new set of teeth when the last ones had been beaten out of her. I had not rescued my niece from her disintegrating mother and her anorexia. The list goes on and on. My parents' failed attempt to rescue everyone was transformed into blame of me for not having done the job.

It was as if each of my family members needed a donated organ and my parents looked to me as the one who could, should and would donate each of the organs. They failed to see the resulting devastation that would cause me, and in fact, seemed to think that I would simply rebound, as I always had, no matter what had been wrenched from me. They imbued me with special powers that I simply did not have.

Like the Murphys, luck played a part in my good fortune, but my mother could not understand or support the hard work, good decisions, and disciplined focus that played a huge role in building my own life. The decisions I made to create my own future, and eventually my own family, were decisions incongruent with rescuing the other members of her family. My mother saw my husband's and my hard-earned salaries as "wealth." But we were not rich at all. We started out our married lives with salaries of $16,000 and $12,000, and a monthly mortgage of $400. What did we do? We rented out a room in the house to help pay the mortgage. Did we hire professional photographers to capture our perfect children dressed in new holiday clothing? No, we took our own photographs of our children in second-hand clothes. Living within our means, my husband and I built a good, although imperfect marriage, and raised two wonderful, although imperfect, children. The best and highest use of my success, as my mother saw it, was to rescue other, more unfortunate members of the family. And I failed to do so.

After a lifetime of fruitless efforts to make repairs to the family in which I had grown up, in my mid-twenties I began an ongoing process of separating myself from family members. I needed to protect myself from their expectations of and disappointment in me. Fulfilling the only familial obligation I felt was required of me, though, I remained as caretaker of my parents until their deaths. I wish I was more able to give myself credit for what most agree is the extraordinary care I provided for them. Mostly I find fault with my impatience and frustration, and the things I didn't do for them. I regret to this day that I did not take my son Daniel to visit my parents when he was dressed as Huck Finn, one of my father's favorite fictional characters, for Halloween. When my parents died, I was unable to cry. By then I had carried their burden for far too long.

As for my other family members, I tried, and from their perspective, failed, to walk the fine line between loving them and keeping my distance from them and their expectations of me. No doubt they would say that I managed only to keep my distance. I did and still do love each of them in the only way I am able.

As Bill wrote, everyone depended on me and had high expectations of me. And why not? For years I had been able to meet, and even exceed, expectations; for years I had given the appearance that I had come through adversity unscathed. My mother had depended on me from my earliest years and she led everyone to think I was unflappable, a rock. My family thought I could handle anything thrown at me. They all thought they could lean on me and berate me for all the things I did wrong or worse, didn't do, and I would never fall over. They were right in one way: I did not fall over, but I did learn that I needed to protect myself from the constant barrage of criticism and never having done enough. I relinquished the dream of unconditional love and support that others get from their families in order to escape the unbearable familial burden I carried.

I wish there could have been a different ending to this story. I dream of different endings. In one, my mother is in a plain linen green A-line dress, beautifully offsetting her red hair in a halo around her as she says, "Bill and I are moving to New York [a city he detested]!" I allow myself to float ideas about my mother and Bill meeting, getting married, and raising me as their child. A happy ending, perhaps in a house in the GE Plot.

The reality, though, is that other possible endings are not guaranteed to be happy ones. Even the ideal scenario, that my mother and Bill met and got married before they were entangled in their families, is an impossible one. I wouldn't be here, writing this memoir today, because I am the result of a love that came about in the circumstances in which they found themselves. I am the result of the pieces they contributed on that day, and not some other day, and I wouldn't be here to tell my story if circumstances had played out differently.

If my mother and Bill had abandoned their families once they met and fell in love, so many others, including spouses and children, would have been impacted. If my mother and Bill had left their spouses at a time when divorce was socially unacceptable and highly unusual, would they have been severed from the children they had with their spouses? Would Bill's career have suffered? I can only imagine Tottie making life miserable for my mother and Bill forever and a day. My father might have imploded, completely depleted, wasted and unable to be the father he was to his children. And I think of the way Tottie doted on Bill, taking care of his every need, arranging life for him in a way that allowed him to focus solely on his work and become a revered academic. I want to believe that my mother would not have allowed herself to serve in the doting role played by Tottie; my mother had too much she wanted to do and to be. In retrospect, though, she compromised so much more and received so little satisfaction in exchange.

Bill's daughter Sue recalls an almost oppressive cheerfulness about my mother during those years when the families spent so much time together. Sue doesn't believe her father could have lived with that on a daily basis. Bill needed space to go to dark and solitary places. Irony abounds. In fact, Bill often spent weeks alone in his study, refusing to engage with Tottie, coming in only when called for dinner. And my memories of my mother are one of a depressed woman who seldom exhibited cheerfulness. Might they both have been more cheerful and engaged if they had been able to be together?

No, any other scenario would have been different but not necessarily better. Instead, we got the very imperfect ending we have. Bad luck dogged the Trumbulls while good fortune shined upon the Murphys. My mother summed up in a letter she wrote to Bill after Jonathan's death, "Tottie seems to gain children and chattels, and I seem to keep losing them."

Only recently did I learn that DNA played a part in my ability to escape the madness of my family. The new DNA knowledge proved to be frosting on the cake of what I had already built. I received the best of the DNA from my mother and my father Bill. The discovery fit perfectly into the life I had already crafted.

As all of this was unfolding, I gradually shared the news with my only remaining brother, Eric. At first I told him about the affair, and my suspicions of my parentage, and later about the results of the DNA test. Years earlier, Eric had done a DNA test, wanting to better understand his ancestry, and said, "I cannot find the Dutch blood. It tells me I am primarily Irish!"

Eric did a new test. He and I share 47% of our DNA which indicates that we have the same mother *and* father. He, too, is Bill's child and my only full sibling. Why didn't he receive from Bill the kind of love and attention that I did? Perhaps Bill simply did not know that Eric was his child. Or perhaps Bill tried to connect with a young Eric who didn't respond the way Bill would have liked. It might simply be the age difference, and that Bill saw me, five years younger than Eric, as particularly vulnerable. Perhaps Bill preferred girls to boys, although I saw him take great pride in his sons throughout his life. As a young adult, Eric took a sharp exit from the Trumbull family, and it may be that Bill also felt that distance and lack of interest in a connection. Bill made several unsuccessful attempts to connect with Eric in later years, a disappointment he shared with me. This DNA news must play completely differently for Eric, who did not receive the wonderful nurturing from Bill that I received. His story is his own to tell. With no answer for why I received the attention while my brother Eric did not, the genetic news confirms my suspicion that the relationship between my mother and Bill went on from soon after they met until I was born, eight years later, if not even longer.

The DNA results also allowed me to confirm the source of some niggling medical issues: two surgeries have not resolved my ongoing sinus issues. Bill told me, in my adulthood, that he had terrible sinuses and an early, botched surgery. When a twin pregnancy of mine failed in the middle trimester, a high platelet count was the initial suspected cause of the miscarriage. "I, too, have a high platelet count," Bill said late in his life, adding, as if trying to assure me that it was insignificant, said, "I won't die from it. Something else will get me first, the doctor tells me." After much testing, a suspected auto-immune disease was eliminated as the cause of the lost pregnancy. In either an ironic twist or a testament to the fallibility of medical science, Sue takes daily medication for the very same auto-immune disease that was suspected and then ruled out as the cause of my lost pregnancy. The shape of my head that disappointed my sister so? Thank you, Bill. My hairy big toe? Bill. And my own awful throat clearing and snorting resulting from my chronic sinus troubles does not sound nearly as erudite as Bill's did. The devastating blood clots and seizures that plagued my father during my teenage years? No longer mine, genetically, to worry about. As is, perhaps, my fear that I too will someday develop the devastating mental illness that plagued my brother and sister.

Growing up, I often blamed my parents for not talking about Peter and his death. We were not allowed to say his name in the house and I wanted, more than anything, to be able to talk about him and what he meant to us, to our family. And it was tragedy redux when Jonathan died. Only now do I understand that if we had begun to talk, the Pandora's box might have opened, one conversation spilling into another, and the whole secret might have been exposed. The secret was kept at all costs. And the costs were great.

The day he told me about my mother and Bill, Chris said, "In the end, what difference does it make?" and in a way, he is right. But now I am able to recall how Bill made me feel like the most wonderful person in the world, as if I came first. And now I know that feeling came to me from the single person, perhaps, who meant the world to me, my father Bill.

And that has made all the difference.

10. Measured Drawings

When they hear even a small part of my life story, people often ask, "How did you turn out to be so OK"?

Sometimes I want to credit Lena, my math teacher in high school, or Mrs. Bornemann, my Spanish professor in college, two teachers who believed in me. But that wasn't it. It took much longer than that for my life to turn around, a process that continues. The emotional scars I have today are not proof of all that went wrong but rather reminders of my strength. Scars, I have learned, contribute to who you are.

I feel lucky to have found a deep inner strength and that I figured out how to reach that strength often. Where did it come from? I attribute it to learning early to set goals. Early in my childhood I saw a future and, brick by brick, built an inner core and carefully constructed that future. I wanted a family and I wanted a career. I learned early the satisfaction of creating and achieving a goal, and that has helped provide me with a framework on which to structure my life. Writing this memoir is a goal I set for myself and in completing it I feel a sense of accomplishment. Only in the eighteenth year of thinking about and finally coming to completion of this story, in my early sixties, did I discover the underlying indisputable truth. The new information I learned finally provided a salve to my emotional scars.

It wasn't my high school math teacher or my college Spanish teacher. My rescue came in the form of a class I took when I began to study the history of architecture in graduate school. The experience allowed me to finally excel and to receive accolades for my work, to be appreciated for who I was rather than berated for who I was not. Not trusting my own mind to philosophize about buildings or design, I did trust my steady hand and attention to detail and learned how to create beautiful architectural drawings. With an architectural drawing, there would be no philosophical argument that I needed to defend, no grammatical tenses I needed to find, no accent where I needed to pull an "r" from the back of my throat. These were the types of things that I could never get right as the younger sister of the older and perfect sister against whom I was always compared. The kind of drawings I mastered were objective and true, the essence of architectural representation. There was a black and whiteness (literally) to them that appealed to me. They required a talent that I considered silly — a steady hand, good eye, and perfectionism — attributes that, because I had them, I would never have considered actual strengths.

The embryonic stages of this love were born in a drafting class in college in which I learned how to create a vanishing point and use Rapid-o-Graph pens in various widths, to their best advantage. That was when my sister stole my new set of pens. Perhaps she saw that I was finally coming into my own and would no longer be under her thumb. Maybe she thought she could stop the process by stealing the pens.

My love of architectural drawing took flight when I began a class in graduate school called "Measured Drawings." I found my place. Never having been concerned with grades, for the first time in my life I felt I deserved the A I received. Utterly enjoying the activity, I worked diligently and produced excellent work. The professor submitted the drawings done by each of his students to the Historic American Buildings Survey (HABS), a program created by an architect named Charles Peterson for unemployed architects during the Depression. All original HABS drawings — thousands of them — are archived at the Library of Congress.

HABS measured drawings are considered the ultimate standard in recording historic buildings. Throughout my career I documented a variety of types of buildings, including the Goyer-Lee House (a prime example of Second Empire Victorian); the Elizabeth Cady Stanton house (a building associated with a person of historic significance); and the Frederick Law Olmsted Home and Office (a site associated with an important body of work in American history).

Typically, a HABS project is substantial in size and requires a team of people, a minimum of two and up to five. The team is often provided housing onsite, or nearby, for a period of months, and spends most waking hours at the site. Drafting boards are set up onsite and a room becomes an office for the duration of the project. With a large project and team, the first step is to divvy up the views of the building — those critical to document the structure and the person who will undertake which drawings. Someone gets to draw the front of the building (a winner), someone gets the back (usually not a winner), and team members select from among the other views.

Long before I was part of an official HABS team, my first set of measured drawings was of a tiny family chapel, the Garth Chapel, in a private cemetery on a country road in Virginia. For this small project, I was able to do most of the work myself, including the initial sketches. I began by creating pencil sketches of each view of the building — front elevation, back elevation, side elevation, a section, or slice through the building to see inside, both longitudinally and transversely. In addition, specific architectural details such as window trim deserve their own drawings, at a large scale, and these were also sketched. With sketches in hand, every aspect of the building is then measured to within an eighth inch, and all measurements are noted on the original pencil sketches. I carefully recorded the measurements, using red pen for measurements going one way on the paper, and blue for measurements going the other direction. This sketch, fully marked up in red and blue, and often dirty and crinkly from sweat having dripped on it during the process, is the foundation for the actual measured drawing.

The detail required of this work is such that, for instance, a stone wall could not be imagined and simply drawn on paper. Each stone had to be measured, with nicks and abnormalities all reflected in the drawings. A process called "stippling" includes the use of thousands of dots added to the paper by the tip of the pen only. This approach reflects the nuances of uneven surfaces with the greater number of dots reflecting a darker spot and a smaller number of dots reflecting a lighter portion. The value of HABS drawings in their painstaking detail, in addition to the historical record they provide, is that they can be used to recreate an important piece of history in painstaking detail, if needed. The Franklin Delano Roosevelt home in Hyde Park, New York was documented by HABS before a fire decimated the structure. It was reconstructed based on the drawings.

While Garth Chapel was so small that I was able to do a lot of the measuring myself, I dragged along friends occasionally to help "hold zero," the phrase for holding one end of the measuring tape. A bond grows between the person undertaking the drawings and the building itself. It becomes an intimate relationship in an odd way. Unlike the ineffable relationship that I had with my mother, the connection with a building is pure and anything but untouchable. I loved spending my Sundays out there on that country road, silent and by myself, measuring and drawing Garth Chapel.

I was grateful by this time to have escaped the immediacy of my family's problems. And yet I desperately clung to an image I had created of a relationship between my mother and me. I allowed myself to recall the carefree moments, the laughter and the singing, our travels together, alone, unburdened by others in the family. I allowed myself to pretend she was a good mother to me. Silent time alone at Garth Chapel and distance from the reality of the situation allowed the fantasy to flourish. But the adult I was becoming recognized that the distance itself was the crucial ingredient that allowed even a semblance of a normal mother-daughter relationship.

It was the crinkly pieces of paper, the wrinkled and crusty chaos, the sweaty paper with red and blue numbers all over them, that became the source of the drawings that would unfold and convey the essence of order. The next stage took place at the drafting table.

There was nothing quite like it: a drafting table with a clean sheet of "mylar," a film with a matte finish that is as smooth as the skin of a baby. Each drawing was fresh, a new beginning, a clean start. It was at that point in the process that I could begin to imagine the clear crisp drawing that would result from my efforts, the transformation of chaos into order. There was no room for error, there was no opportunity for something that might not belong to interject itself, nor was there room for someone who didn't behave to enter the scene. The processing of drawing was clean, exact, and unburdened. In my little apartment in Charlottesville, no one came along to tell me my French accent wasn't quite right, or that I really wasn't smart enough to do this work. Finding measured drawings was the way I discovered that I am capable. My ability to transform chaos into order ultimately allowed me to believe I could do the same with my life.

First I put a record on the stereo and then I sat down at my drafting table with its "Mayline," a bar attached to the table that would slide up and down to ensure proper horizontal and vertical alignment. A lamp with a flexible arm attached to the drafting table allowed me to focus light on the specific location where I was drawing, something akin to a dentist's light that zeros in on your teeth. I taped the corners of the mylar to the drafting table surface, a clean film of vinyl that served as an underlying surface which allowed the pen to flow smoothly. My pens sat beside me, clean and ready for inking when the final stage of the process would begin. But for the penciling stage, a lead holder and graphite served as my tool. An electric sharpener was at the ready because each pencil line needed to be perfectly consistent and required sharp lead. A sliver thin sheet of metal, called an erasing shield, allowed me to erase a mistake without doing damage to any other line on the drawing. I used a special brush to sweep off any dust or eraser detritus. Various triangles were placed tight against the Mayline horizontal base to provide a perfectly perpendicular vertical line. Curves required intensive measuring and a tool known as a "flexible curve" to recreate the exact geometry of the curve. As I worked, the building I had measured the day before began to take on new life in the form of a drawing. I often stood back, brushed the paper clean of any dust that might have settled, and admired the drawing that was unfolding before me, first tilting my head one way and then the other. The chaos was becoming order.

I stayed up late into the night, my best work often done between ten and one in the morning, in the silence of the night with only my music playing. I forgot to eat or drink and I thought of nothing but the drawing and what line I should undertake next, always keeping the future product in my mind's eye. When complete, it was beautiful. Each drawing needs to line up perfectly with the drawing to which it is related. An elevation, or front façade, must line up perfectly with the floor plan to which it is related — the width of the façade must match perfectly with the width of that wall on the floor plan. Across all drawings, everything must line up perfectly.

The next stage of the process was even better.

With a complete and accurate set of penciled drawings, I then began the drawing process over again, but this time with ink. The drafting table was swept and cleaned, the penciled drawing taped to the table, the

Little As You Were

drawing itself swept with the brush, and, once again, with music on, I sat at the table to draw. I taped the corners of the fresh mylar sheet over the pencil drawing, placing the framed mylar appropriately over the pencil drawing to center it visually.

Sweeping the table once more, I began. The cleanliness of the work space was essential to the creation of the drawing and also to the clarity of my mind. I could not allow any interference, in the way of dust, eraser rubbings, or phone calls from anyone in my family. From my new and expanded set of Rapido-o-graph pens, the very kind my sister had stolen from me many years before, I selected the thickest width pen to outline the building, to help "pop" the building out from the background. It is one way of giving a slight hint of depth to a two-dimensional drawing. Often I started by touching my pen end to my finger to begin the flow of ink. The resulting lines all over my fingers soon became known as "HABS hairs;" they became daily temporary scars in service of the ultimate beauty. I was able to stop the pen with utmost precision to keep the ink from pooling and causing a bulbous bulge at the end of the line. I carefully studied the interior lines in order to use the correct width pen for each of the lines, further providing a sense of depth. I seldom sang along to the music, which would have been my natural inclination, because I didn't want anything to affect my steadiness. As the music played, lines appeared on the page, one line after another, until the drawing was, to me, the embodiment of perfection. The finished product was magnificent. I used a Leroy lettering guide to identify the drawing, its artist, and other critical information using the only font HABS allowed.

The Goyer-Lee house

A single measured drawing can take hours or days. A full set of measured drawings can take weeks or months. The drawing of the front façade of the Goyer-Lee House shown here took me forty hours to pencil and another forty hours to ink.

The very act of producing measured drawings was heaven to me. Throughout the process I became increasingly committed to the importance of each line I drew in permanent ink. Each one was a critical part of the drawing and deserved a place on the page. And with every line I inked, I became more and more convinced that I, too, deserved a place in this world, a footprint on this earth.

I had found my niche. I was wildly successful. Eventually my drawings were chosen as covers of magazines, for publication in architecture books, and for posters advertising special moments in the history of the *Historic American Buildings Survey*. They were made into note cards for a bed and breakfast that was created out of a building I documented.

But early on, after my very first attempt at a set of measured drawings, peers, co-workers and teachers commended me for my work. Soon I was selected to take an independent study in measured drawings. Not long after, when Colonial Williamsburg asked, I was the person recommended for a job creating measured drawings. Following that, came a job with the National Park Service, home to the *Historic American Buildings Survey*, to serve on a team doing measured drawings of the Frederick Law Olmsted Home and Office in Brookline, Massachusetts. The supervisor on that job was a young man who eventually became my husband, and that job led to a position in the HABS mothership office in Washington, D.C., and a role as supervisor of a team doing drawings of a plantation home in Tidewater, Virginia. That led to an offer from the Mid-Atlantic region of the National Park Service overseeing all the HABS work done in the region. In Philadelphia, Charles Peterson, who created the HABS program during the Depression, attended the wedding of my husband and me, two HABS kids. In retrospect it turns out I was in the right place at the right time, and my measured drawings were one of the last batches completed before computers took over. But in that moment, my moment, I finally received recognition for the activity that delighted me unabashedly.

The *Historic American Buildings Survey* now records buildings using computer technology and computer printing. But at one time, HABS required the talent of detail-oriented people like me and I made a name for myself. I wasn't second to anyone. I was the best.

In addition to the admittedly compulsive attention to detail required for measured drawings, the study of architectural history provided me a new and more sophisticated way to love and understand spaces. Buildings intrigued me: vernacular buildings — barns, smokehouses, outhouses, summer kitchens — in the rolling hills of Virginia; the clarity and perfect symmetry of Brunelleschi's Pazzi Chapel in Florence, Italy; and the clean lines of the mid-century skyscrapers of Chicago. Always imagining how a set of drawings would unfold, I also learned anew the impact that a physical environment can have on a person. I became convinced that I could create space for my life, the life I had only recently become convinced I deserved to live. My study of architectural history allowed me to take charge of my life. I would determine my own path, what I thought, and how I felt. I would create my own destiny, the architecture of my life. You might say that buildings — and architecture — saved my life and allowed me to become the person I am today.

I did just that. I created my own spaces and my own destiny. After the house on Hirtle Island, I made a home out of my little apartment in Charlottesville while in graduate school, and then a series of houses — some Victorian, some early twentieth century — as I built my family. I continue to create spaces and my destiny. The spaces I create are always free of clutter, free of angst, and finally, free of blood.

Epilogue

Years ago, when I sent Bill the chapter of this memoir about Peter's death, he responded immediately, saying he would call as soon as he could stop crying. I was certain at the time that he was crying at the memory of that awful day and perhaps, even, with the way I portrayed it through the eyes of a six-year-old. All that might be true, but he was also crying because one of his children was a writer. I recalled Bill's pride about my one day publishing a book (or two or three). I relish the irony that the first and only (no doubt) book I will ever publish is one that unravels the very story he and my mother went to such lengths to conceal.

My mother's breast cancer returned when she was eighty-six. By then she was blind. Together she and I chose not to treat the cancer and to instead let her live out her final days in the comfort of her blue chair in the nursing home, in the room she shared with her husband. She died soon after we refused treatment. The single phone call I made when I learned she had died was not to my father. No, the only phone call I made, and perhaps for solace, was to Bill. "My mother has died, Bill," I said. The other end of the phone got silent, and I knew that he was crying that familiar way men often do, choking to muffle any possibility of really crying.

Five days after my mother died, my father came down with pneumonia, what Bill called "an old man's best friend." Knowing it would bring on his death, for which he was ready, I declined treatment. He died five days later.

One of the last things my father said before he stopped talking, was "Bet and I are going to the lake." He meant Lake George, and, a year or so later, family members gathered for the send-off of my parents' ashes on bark boats on a quiet calm October evening.

Lake George. The most special place in the world: the place that we all waited for, dreamt of, longed for, year after year. The lake where Bill came to visit my family and wrote to me in a letter years later, "…you took my hand and led me about on that island when you were two or three. In the normal order of things I should have been leading you about… And the wonderful talk that poured forth from your sweet voice, full of observation and philosophy…"

Bettina and Daniel, young

Today, my son Daniel VanVechten and my daughter Bettina join us at Lake George every summer, a tradition that began when my son was three, although we no longer camp on the islands. We still launch bark boats when the evening lake is calm enough. Now we use birthday candles that automatically relight until they have burned down to the bottom. We sit on the dock and sing songs — sometimes *Grandfather's Clock, Erie Canal or the Titanic,* the songs my father — well, Van — used to sing to me at bedtime, while we watch the candles flicker, sometimes losing their light and then lighting up again, as the stars begin to come out.

Bettina and Daniel, young adults

www.ingramcontent.com/pod-product-compliance
Lightning Source LLC
Chambersburg PA
CBHW041353290426
44108CB00006B/131